Alpha & Omega:
The Beginning of the End

An Introduction to
the End Times

Kameel Majdali

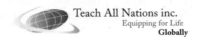

Teach All Nations inc.
Equipping for Life
Globally

www.tan.org.au

Teach All Nations Inc.
P.O. Box 493
Mount Waverley, Victoria 3149
AUSTRALIA

ISBN: 0 9775345 0 2

Teach All Nations Inc. is a Bible teaching ministry that seeks to equip people for life globally. For more information about the services and resources of Teach All Nations Inc., contact us at our website:

www.tan.org.au

Preface

It is a subject that fascinates and frightens, inflames and inspires, tears down yet builds up. Theologians call it "Eschatology," but it simply means the doctrine of last things. Eschatology is not just an interesting subject, but it is vital for your spiritual growth, too.

Eschatology has waxed and waned in favor over the years. During the second half of the twentieth century, it caught the imagination of the church world and even the secular world, with so many significant events happening in Europe and the Middle East. By the end of the twentieth century, with the advent of postmodernism and the overuse and abuse of prophetic teaching, Bible prophecy was pushed to the side and neglected. By its very nature, however, it is impossible for this subject to stay in the shadows. Eschatology will rise again.

The Doctrine of Last Things is crucial for our understanding and success in our relationship with God. This author, having taught the subject at Bible college and tertiary level for many years, has endeavored to write a simple, straight-forward guide to introduce the beginner, and the serious Bible student, to the wonderful world of eschatology.

The very nature of Eschatology, with its "valid uncertainties," means that no one will agree with everything that is written. But in a spirit of Christian charity, with a noble Berean mindset to search the Scriptures daily to see if these things are so, Alpha and Omega seeks to give you a framework in which to do further study and to grow in grace.

Learning Eschatology will not only protect you from the soon-coming spirit of error, but also give you great hope in a age of increasing nihilism. The more sure word of prophecy truly is a light that shines in a dark place.

- Kameel Majdali
  Melbourne, Australia

Contents

Dedication

To my family and friends
who stood with me
during this important transition
from Rehoboth to Beersheba.

Part One

Introduction

Chapter One

Why Prophecy? Why Now?

We should all be concerned about the future because we will have to spend the rest of our lives there—C.F. Kettering

A Best-Seller

He was a former tugboat operator in New Orleans who attended the heartland of American dispensational teaching, Dallas Theological Seminary. This man then wrote a book that spoke about World War III, nuclear holocaust, and a Russian invasion of Israel. Published in 1970, the book sold over 28 million copies and became the subject of a 1978 documentary narrated by Orson Welles, who also did "war of the worlds." The author was Hal Lindsey and his book was called *The Late Great Planet Earth*. Lindsey took the massive topic of Bible prophecy and popularized it, sometimes with folksy language (e.g. Scarlet O'Harlot), and it ended up being a runaway best seller.

Thus one of the top-selling single volumes of all time--next to the Bible itself which is the all-time best-seller year after year--was devoted to prophecy. Another series of best-sellers, called Left Behind, is also related to the end-times. In our fallen, double-minded world, we can be either apathetic or terrified by prophecy but also simultaneously captivated by it as well.

You are about to be introduced to a wonderful subject called "Eschatology," a branch of theology which deals with the doctrine of last things: last days, last events, and even what happens to people when they die. The amount of ignorance and misinformation about Eschatology is enormous. What you will learn is that a proper knowledge, even if rudimentary, will help you to understand the times, give you direction, and bring old-fashioned blessings.

Only a few years ago, the subject of Eschatology was often the most popular subject in Bible schools and churches. Bible teachers and evangelists specialized in this topic, both to the delight and dread of many. Some were self-appointed "watchmen on the walls." Bible prophecy was big business but also a volatile one. In more recent times, however, the watchman has been in danger of being retrenched.

Bible Prophecy: In Danger from Friend and Foe

Why has such a fascinating and important subject like end-times fallen on hard times? Why are more and more churches avoiding this subject? How could something that was once so revered be so scorned?

For one, there are several different eschatological views, like amillennialism and premillenialism, which can be contradictory and confusing to the average Christian. People have enough trouble trying to balance their cheque book, let alone unscramble the eschatological egg.

Date-setting has posed other problems. It has caused people to defer having a family, planning for the future, buying a home, or living a normal life. Some of these have sold up homes, quit their jobs, stored up freeze-dried food, and retreated into the wilderness to wait for the end. By all accounts, they are still waiting!

Many false alarms have been sounded over the years, stating that Jesus was returning very soon. One man wrote a book called "Eighty-eight Reasons Why Jesus is Returning in 1988." This book caused a big stir in many circles. At that time this author was a pastor in a local church and remembered the mild anxiety that some members of the congregation had at the prospect of Jesus returning that year. One man lamented, "I can't afford to have the Lord return this year; I am too busy!" My response was quick and simple: "When you are too busy for Jesus to return, then you are too busy!"

When 1988 passed into history without Jesus returning, apparently a sequel was published with the predictable title "Eighty-Nine Reasons Why...." The unbiblical practice of date-setting has caused enormous damage to the cause of Christ, making even Christians skeptical about the imminent coming of the LORD.

It is not only the friends of eschatology that can "love it to death," but also the enemies too. During the heady times of the Reagan and Clinton administrations, when the US economy and stock market were riding high like a Hawaiian wave, people did not want to hear any "doom and gloom" messages. These are postmodern times and messages of tribulation and judgement are replaced with therapeutic motivational messages to help people "feel good" about themselves. Now is the time to make money, they say.

Even in Bible colleges, Eschatology has been demoted from a required subject to an elective. A few years ago, a Bible college student in his 40's came to this author in the first days of the Eschatology class. He made the following comment:

"Does it matter if Jesus comes before the Great Tribulation or after? Does it matter if there is a Millennium or not? I just want to win souls and plant churches! Does Bible prophecy really matter?"

The short answer is simple: Yes--absolutely yes.

Core of Scripture

We also have the prophetic word made more sure, which you do well to heed as a light that shines in a dark place, until the day dawns and the morning star rises in your hearts—II Peter 1:19 NKJV

Paramount among all the reasons for the relevance and indispensability of Bible prophecy is the fact that **at least one-quarter to one-third of Scripture is devoted to the future**. The Old Testament provides us with five Major and twelve Minor Prophets, all of whom provide light about the end of the age (not counting prophet utterances in the Law and the Writings). Prophecy is scattered throughout the New Testament, but culminates in the Book of Revelation.

Consider some of the Bible's track record in prophetic utterances thus far:

- The prophet Jeremiah predicted Judah would go into captivity to Babylon for seventy years (Jeremiah 25:11-12) but eventually it would return to its land. It was not the norm for exiled people to make a comeback to their homeland; however, Jeremiah was so confident that the Jews would come back to the land that he bought the field of Anathoth near the capital during the final successful Babylonian siege on Jerusalem. This purchase was a prophetic act and a statement of faith. Seventy years later, the Jews did return and were even supported by the Medo-Persian Emperor.

- Isaiah said Israel would be sent home by the Persians and mentioned the name of the benefactor Cyrus (Ezra 1:1; Isaiah 44:28) one hundred and fifty years before the event;

- Daniel saw the vision of four Gentile empires, Babylon, Persia, Greek, Roman-Imperial (Daniel 2 & 7); all four of these empires have come to the world scene and their legacies still continues to influence civilization unto this day.

- The prophet Micah predicted that Bethlehem in Judah would be the birthplace of Israel's Messiah. Furthermore, he alluded to the Messiah's pre-existence (Micah 5:2), which implies His divinity as well.

- Daniel predicted when the Messiah would appear and the fact that he would be "cut off" (or killed, crucified) in Daniel 9:24-27 (known as the Seventy Week Prophecy). It is very clear that the Messiah had to show up before the Jerusalem Temple was destroyed in A.D. 70. Try using this passage when witnessing to your Jewish friends. The Seventy Week prophecy was instrumental in the conversion of Jewish insurance agent Stan Telchin; a story eloquently recounted in his book Betrayed.

- Jesus predicts destruction of the Temple, which happened in AD 70 (Luke 21:6).

- Over three hundred prophecies speak about the first coming of Jesus, and all of them have come to pass literally and completely. These prophecies go into detail on major aspects of His life, including the virgin birth (Isaiah 7:14), the manner of His death with His hands and feet pierced (Psalm 22:16), and His resurrection (Psalm 16:10).

The Hebrew prophets had an accuracy rate of one hundred percent. To disregard Bible prophecy is to blind ourselves to one-third of God's Word and arguably the most important third of all. If we can trust the prophecies regarding the first coming of Christ, we can clearly accept prophecies surrounding the second coming. That is why Peter says a more sure word of prophecy is a light that shines in a dark place.

Why Study Prophecy?

By definition, prophecy means knowledge of the future given by divine revelation. Another way of explaining it is the declaration of the future under divine inspiration. While there is a "forth telling" aspect to prophecy, thus conveying information not known by natural means, the main emphasis has to be that which is detailed and predictive about the future. More specifically, it is God's declaration of what He has planned for the times ahead. Most of the time, the prophesied event will require divine intervention in order to come to pass. In other words, it will be a time of the supernatural and miraculous.

In answer to the above question of the sincere yet skeptical student—does prophecy matter—remember that the study of prophecy offers many benefits, as you will see below.

Light of the Word

Just as Jesus Christ is the "Light of the World" (John 8:12) prophecy enables the "light of the Word" to shine on our lives. Psalm 119:105 declares "Your word is a lamp to my feet and a light to my path." Proverbs 4:18 tells us that the "path of the just" is as a shining light that shines more brightly until the "perfect day."

> *To disregard Bible prophecy is to blind ourselves to one-third of God's Word and arguably the most important third of all.*

One thing to bear in mind about the "last days' is that they are not all about 'doom and gloom." Yes, there will be dangers and challenges all around. Life will become more intense and its pace will accelerate. But the righteous are promised that they will never be in darkness but have the light of life (John 8:12). As they proceed towards their future on the path of the just, they will not be in darkness; on the contrary, the light will get brighter and brighter until the perfect day when Jesus returns.

Likewise, Isaiah 60:1-2 is an excellent example of the chasm-like contrasts in the last days. The earth will be enveloped in darkness and even "gross darkness" shall cover people. So gross, in fact, that even grown men will cry out in terror because of their fear of the dark. But at this very time when the world system is becoming darker and darker, the Lord's light will become brighter and brighter on His righteous ones. More specifically, what is the source of this light in God's Word? Prophecy is probably the brightest aspect of the light of God's Word.

In these days of complexity, contrast, contravention, and confusion, the light of prophecy cuts a clear pathway for the righteous to walk. In II Peter 1:19-21 it says that we as Christian believers have "a more sure word of prophecy" and we would be well advised to listen to the prophetic word. Why? The metaphor is that it is a light that shines in a dark place. Anyone who is stuck in a tunnel or is trapped in a cave would enthusiastically welcome any bit of light they could find, if only to help them get out. The "more sure word of prophecy" does precisely that: showing us how to

15

navigate through the varied and challenging situations in third millennium living.

Furthermore, Peter exhorts us to keep listening to the "word of prophecy" until the day dawns and the daystar arises in our hearts. This means that until Jesus Christ returns to this planet, prophecy is the best light we have; indeed, prophecy is God's means of providing us the brightest and most secure search light until Christ's light shines down on us. It is God's will that you know the future (Deuteronomy 29:29; Amos 3:7). Through prophecy you learn that the dead will be resurrected, Jesus Christ will return to earth, and we who belong to Him will live with Him forever. It truly is the light that shines in a dark place.

Major Portion of the Bible

As already mentioned, prophecy comprises a major part of God's Word. Estimates vary from one-fourth to one-third. People who avoid the prophetic parts of Scripture are losing out on an incalculable portion of Scripture and, arguably the most important portion, because it tells us about the future we hope to have. More to the point, it helps us to prepare for this God-designed future. Frankly, those who avoid prophecy are sleepwalking into the future, which is a most dangerous habit. Sleepwalkers may be active but they don't know where they are going and the possibility of injury or worse is very great. But those who embrace the prophetic word are wide-awake, focused, and poised to receive God's best.

Affirms Christ and the Bible

Prophecy affirms, validates, and vindicates the Lord Jesus Christ and the Holy Bible that so faithfully attests to Him. Remember that there are hundreds of prophecies about Christ that have been fulfilled to the letter during His first coming. Though a few skeptics have tried to make these fulfilled prophecies look like a "set-up," it is virtually impossible to sustain such a claim. How could Christ arrange the place of His birth, the time and manner of His death, or His own resurrection, which included liberation from the grave clothes, rolling away a heavy stone from the doorway, and walking out of His own tomb? Though Christ was renowned for His miraculous ministry, without question the greatest miracle of all was His resurrection from the dead.

> *We can confidently take a high view of Scripture, including all the miracles, supernatural events, and prophecies, because Jesus Christ, the Risen Lord, Believed these things too.*

Scripture also stands validated because of the prophetic word. Major prophetic fulfillments have occurred like the seventy-year captivity of the Jews in Babylon, the rise of Cyrus the Great (by name), Nebuchadnezzar's statue which represents four gentile empires, and the destruction of Herod's Temple in A.D. 70.

Christ had a very high and conservative view about Scripture. He believed in it from Genesis to Malachi--the New Testament had not been written yet--including the prophecies and miracles. Because of His own sinless life and powerful resurrection, He has the credibility to give unqualified endorsement to the whole of the Scriptures. We can therefore believe in the supernatural aspects of Scripture, as well as prophecies, simply because the Risen Christ believed in them, too.

A Call to Righteousness

Prophecy is more than just predicting the future. It is a reflection of God's holy character and a call to repentance and righteousness. Micah 6:8 says that God has shown what He requires of us: to do justice, love mercy, and walk humbly with Him. When people understand prophecy, it can have a sobering effect which causes them to revise their lifestyle in alignment to God's Word.

It is like the teenagers who were minding the house while their parents were away. When the parents delayed their return, the teenagers became slack. Inviting their friends for late-night celebrations, they would live as if there was no tomorrow. The party is on! Their friends have come like vultures to the carcasses, the music is blasting, the sink is loaded with dishes, and the appearance of the home is in total disarray. Then they receive an unexpected phone call: the parents are coming home early; in fact, they are on their way. Everything changes: the friends are expelled, the rubbish is removed, and the dishes are washed. A consciousness of God's coming visitation and Christ's return will also bring sobriety and sense to our lives, too.

Jesus speaks about the last days as resembling the "days of Noah." While it is business as usual for those in the world, the people of God are securing their future by the building of the ark. Holiness, repentance, righteousness, acceptable worship, become central in the lives of those who let the light of prophecy shine on them.

Evangelism Fostered

> *There is nothing like a vision of hell to set our feet on the gospel road.*

Prophecy can galvanize the instincts of the would-be evangelist. There is nothing like a vision of hell to set our feet on the gospel road. A member of the cults put a challenge to Bible-believing Christians: if I really believed that there is a hell, full of fire and brimstone, to which there is no escape, I would spend the rest of my life warning everyone I met to flee from the wrath to come. I would not stop until I dropped dead!

Remember that while the people on the doomed ship Titanic were sleeping, eating, partying and playing—and the band played to the end-- the watchmen on the deck were the only ones to see the upcoming iceberg. Had the situation been different: a different speed, a different angle, a different route, a different direction, a different attitude, then everyone could have been saved. But due to the lack of preparedness, impact with the iceberg meant a sure and swift demise. Time was short. They had less than three hours from the time of the collision to when the ship would sink into the frigid dark waters of the North Atlantic. In this time, they had to get as many people into the lifeboats—women and children first— as was possible. Tragically, there were not enough lifeboats, there were no drills, and many boasts were only half filled.[1]

Evangelism means rescuing as many people from doomed world order, which has already struck the iceberg, into the lifeboats of salvation. It is only those who get into the lifeboats who will arrive at their destination.

---

[1]NOTE: the analogy of the Titanic will be used more than once, since it is an easily recognized and readily identifiable parable of the last days.

Peter utilized Bible prophecy from Joel 2:28-32 and Psalm 16:8-11; 68:18, and 110:1 when he preached his powerful Pentecost Day message in Acts 2:14-29. The result was that three thousand souls were added to the newly born Christian church. Philip the Evangelist used Isaiah 53:7-8 when he preached to the Ethiopian eunuch in Acts 8:26-39. While the eunuch was the only one to be evangelized and born again in this instance, tradition tells us that he was the one who brought the message of the Gospel to his home country of Ethiopia, an African country which has had a strong Christian tradition since the very early days of the church.

Even evangelists of our day have used Bible prophecy as the bait to come to God. So in all the above situations, Bible prophecy becomes a powerful and magnetic tool to bring people into a saving knowledge of the Lord Jesus Christ. Prophecy is the light that leads us out of darkness.

REVIEW QUESTIONS:

1. Why is Bible prophecy threatened by both friends and foes?
2. Give a definition of prophecy in your own words.
3. What are the five reasons to study Bible prophecy?

Chapter Two

Signs of the Times?

For people who have a good knowledge of both history and current events, there is no mistaking that we are living in unique and significant times. Consider the following:

The Rise of Globalization

This is the process whereby goods, services, capital, people, information and ideas flow across national boundaries and lead to greater integration and interdependence of nation states, economically, politically, culturally and spiritually. International trade and the exchange of cultural ideas are increasing enormously. Advancements in technology and travel are creating one "global village." Thomas Friedman, author of The Lexus and the Olive Tree, says that globalization first happened in the nineteenth century, but was interrupted by the First World War. This was followed by the "Roaring Twenties," the Great Depression, the Second World War, and the Cold War.

After the collapse of the Berlin Wall in 1989, the second attempt of globalization was unleashed. The demise of communism in Europe, the conversion of the economy of Communist China into de facto capitalism and the arrival of the internet propelled globalization. With the attempt of nation states to join regional "clubs" like the European Union (EU), North American Free Trade Association (NAFTA), the Asia Pacific Economic

Cooperation (APEC), and the move to make the "United Nations" evolve from merely a peace-keeping organization into a base of global governance, globalization is in full swing. Could all this be a prelude to a one-world government, as prophesied by Daniel?

Technological Revolution

Time-saving devices, satellites, global positioning systems, mass travel, fiber optics, computer technology and adventures in cyberspace have changed the way we live forever. Knowledge is doubling at an astronomical rate. Up to the mid-1960's British migrants paid only ten pound sterling to sail to Australia but had to endure six weeks on the ship. Today, the plane flight is only a day away. Is this a fulfillment of Daniel 12:4 which says *"...many shall run to and fro, and knowledge shall increase."*

Does the rise of technology give us the opportunity to see Matthew 24:14 come to pass that *"...this gospel of the kingdom will be preached in all the world as a witness to all the nations, and then the end will come."* More ominously, can it help bring to pass that what was spoken about in Revelation 11:9 about the murder of the two witnesses at Jerusalem *"Then those from the peoples, tribes, tongues, and nations will see their dead bodies three and a half days..."*?

Israel and the Middle East

This is the region where history and civilization began; where the patriarchs, prophets, priests, kings, Messiah, and apostles of the Bible lived and served. Until the book of Acts, all of the Biblical narrative occurred in the Middle East. Furthermore, it is believed that just as time began in this place, so it will end. In Acts 3:19-21 Peter confidently declared that Jesus Christ

> *Could globalization be a prelude to a one-world government, as prophesied by Daniel?*

will come again to this planet, but before He does, all things will be restored as prophesied by the holy prophets since the world began.

The Greek word for "restoration" is *apokatastasis*, which means to restore to its original condition or to its rightful owner. It is like a chessboard that has had all its pieces swept away, only to have them dutifully placed in their original position.

While some Bible teachers teach about an end-time restoration of Israel, there are even more things to be restored than just the Jewish state. One of the things to be restored is Babylon, which has approximately seven chapters in both testaments dedicated to the topic of its ultimate destruction. Then there is the "legs of iron, feet of iron and clay" found in Nebuchadnezzar's statue in the Book of Daniel, which represents the Roman or Imperial Empire.

The fact is that the Middle East today, once a backwater of the Ottoman (Turkish) Empire, has emerged as the Number One headline maker and foreign policy concern for every major government. With Middle East countries eagerly restoring archaeological sites to their ancient glory—e.g. the Pharos lighthouse and library of Alexandria, Egypt; the great Persian cities of Iran; Babylon in Iraq; as well as the cities, language, and culture of ancient Israel—could we actually be seeing a "restored" Middle East in a similar context to what it was like in the first century A.D.? And is this restoration a prelude to the second coming of Jesus? Are "Bible days" here again?

Jerusalem

Though located in the Middle East, Jerusalem deserves separate coverage of its own. The ancient city of Jebus was captured by King David around the year 1,000 B.C. and transformed into Israel's national capital and Yahweh's holy city. Thus Jerusalem became known as the "City of David" and "City of God." When God gave David an everlasting covenant that promised him an heir and everlasting dynasty, his city was transformed into the "City of the Great King." God faithfully preserved Jerusalem, even through its many partial and total destructions, because of His covenant with David. Zechariah prophesied that Jerusalem will become a burdensome stone for all peoples, and that those who tampered with her would be grievously injured. Eventually the nations will invade Judah and Jerusalem.

For many centuries after the New Testament era, Jerusalem has been an inconsequential and little-noticed village in the Judean hills. It would hardly be the material for international concern or controversy. But all of that has changed. Today, the question of "who owns Jerusalem" or the "Jerusalem Question" is the number one foreign policy issue. It has been said that from 1945 to 1990 Jerusalem, Israel, and Palestine have been the content of one-third of all United Nations resolutions. At least sixty different proposals have been made over the twentieth century to solve the Jerusalem Question, but some aspect of each proposal was objectionable between one or more of the parties. Remember, Jerusalem is not just an issue between Israel and the Palestinian Arabs; The United Nations, the Arab world, the Muslim world, the Orthodox Church, the Vatican, the United States, European Union, and Russia are all parties who have a vested interest in the Holy City. Is all this international attention leading to the final cataclysm that Zechariah foretold?

The European Union

Established by the Maastricht Treaty in 1992, the European Union is a supranational and intragovernmental union of twenty-seven European nations (in 2007). With more countries lining up to join, it is headed towards the formation of a European super state. While there have been many attempts in history to unite Europe, including Napoleon and Hitler, this latest move seems to be holding strong.

Is there a prophetic fulfillment in this? Daniel 2 speaks of Nebuchadnezzar's statue, which represents four major world empires from Daniel's day until the second coming of the Messiah. The last of these empires is normally called "The Roman Empire," but the outstanding Hebrew Christian scholar Arnold Fruchtenbaum suggests the term "Imperial Empire" instead. If the latter day Imperial Empire resembles the Roman Empire, then the EU could be a good candidate. The Old Roman Empire encompassed much of Europe, North Africa, and the Middle East. The EU encompasses most of Europe and has received applications from Turkey, which is in Asia Minor and the Middle East, and Morocco in North Africa. Israel has also hinted on a membership possibility. Though enlargement outside of Europe seems unlikely at the moment, this could all change and we could truly have a "revived Imperial Empire," as some Bible teachers interpret.

Famines, Pestilences, and Earthquakes

These are considered "signs of the times" yet it needs to be acknowledged that none of these are new. All of them are found in the Bible and also in post-Biblical history all the way to our time. Where they become prophetically significant is in frequency, intensity, and devastation.

As one example, the Spanish Flu pandemic of 1918-1919 was credited for having caused anywhere from 20 to 40 million deaths; and this occurred on the heels of the end of the First World War, with its casualty rate in the millions. Talk of SARS, Avian Bird Flu, or some other future pandemic, speaks of a death rate far higher, simply because the population has increased.

World Wars

In the Olivet Discourse Jesus makes the prediction that "nation shall rise against nation" and "kingdom against kingdom." The implication is that of armed conflict. Warfare is as old as human existence and we have probably lost count of how many wars there have been since the beginning of recorded history.

But a new dimension to warfare came into being in the twentieth century: world war. Until then, war was between two realms or, at most, two regions. But in 1914, the assassination in Sarajevo Bosnia of the heir of the Austro-Hungarian Empire led to a global conflagration that even pulled in Australia and New Zealand. Not only was the catchment area large but so were the casualties: ten million dead in the First World War and fifty-five million dead in the Second. If Jesus' above mentioned phrase is a Hebrew idiom for a world war, then the last century has introduced to us a frightening dimension with the possibility of total global destruction.

Worldwide Destruction

Again, alluding to the Olivet Discourse, Jesus speaks about how all flesh could be destroyed except for divine intervention, namely, His Second

Coming. Until the twentieth century, the possibility of destroying all life on the planet did not exist. Things have changed with the advent of the nuclear age. The dropping of the atomic bomb on Hiroshima and Nagasaki in 1945, destructive as it was, would easily be eclipsed by the fire-power we have today. This is not including the introduction of weapons of mass destruction, like chemical and bacteriological weaponry. And the Boxing Day 2004 Indian Ocean Tsunami, which killed a quarter of a million people in an instant, proved that natural disasters are still more potent than any manmade device deployed so far.

Pitfalls to Avoid

Someone once said that moderation is simply that midway point as our personal pendulum swings from one extreme to another. This applies to prophecy as to anything else. Some people love prophecy so much that they try to find a prophetic fulfillment in everything they see. Others are either so apathetic or antagonistic that they write off the entire thing as too hard or confusing. It is time to stop the pendulum and to hear what the Holy Spirit is saying to the churches:

> *...of the children of Issachar who had understanding of the times, to know what Israel ought to do...*— *I Chronicles 12:32* KJV

In this day, more than ever, wisdom and understanding are our lifeline and a diligent search of God's Word will make you healthier, wealthier, and wiser. Remember that true prophecy is a light that shines in a dark place until Christ comes again for His people. To ignore it is to remain in a place where increasing darkness will be your only companion.

The Great and Universal Shaking

Hebrews 12:25-26 (NKJV)
25 See that you do not refuse Him who speaks. For if they did not escape who refused Him who spoke on earth, much more shall we not escape if we turn away from Him who speaks from heaven, 26 whose voice then shook the earth; but now He has promised, saying, "Yet once more I shake not only the earth, but also heaven.

Matthew 24:29 (NKJV)
29 Immediately after the tribulation of those days the sun will be darkened, and the moon will not give its light; the stars will fall from heaven, and the powers of the heavens will be shaken.

Like a weatherman scanning the skies, so the last days will have certain telltale signs for those who are watching. One of the greatest has to do with what we call the "universal shaking." Like a gigantic earthquake, this shaking will involve both heaven and earth, so that all "shakeable" or temporal things will be removed.

In many ways, it is the birth pangs of the coming Kingdom: the shakeable kingdoms of this world, represented by Nebuchadnezzar's statue of Daniel 2, will be struck and shaken by the stone cut out of the mountains without hands. The statue, representing the Babylonian, Persian, Hellenistic, and Roman/Imperial Empires--whose legacies are still with us to this day-- will crumble under the might of the stone, until it is no more than a pile of dust. The wind then comes and blows the pile away, until there remains no trace of the statue or empires. The only thing left is the stone which caused the shaking. With all eyes on it, the stone begins to grow and becomes a great mountain that fills the whole earth. This stone is none other than Christ and His Kingdom, which shall never end (Luke 1:33).

In other words, the universal shaking causes the fulfillment of Revelation 11:15, where the "kingdoms of this world" become the Kingdom of Our Lord and Christ. However, unlike the smooth transfer of power after a democratic election, the outgoing empires will not royally welcome this Kingdom. They will need to be ejected forcibly.

> *For the first time in history, we have the potential to destroy all life on earth. This, too, was prophesied long ago in Scripture.*

Beginning with the twentieth century, history has entered into an unprecedented period of universal shaking. Events now are no longer just local or regional, but global in impact. The shakeable kingdoms of this world include the present world system, which is fraught with limitations, anxiety, and hard-to-solve problems. It has a form of glory that, as any celebrity can tell you, quickly fades. Even the well-intentioned religious systems can be part of the world system, degenerating into legalism, religiosity, and bondage.

The reason for this fragility and vulnerability of our world system is well described by the Prophet Isaiah in Chapter 40:6-8: all flesh, meaning all humankind, is grass and all its loveliness is like the flower of the field. Flesh can be attractive one day, but brown, dry, and dead the next. Indeed, the Spirit of the Lord is the cause of the demise of this "flowery" flesh because He blows upon it. Thus even the breath of the Spirit instigates shaking and removal of the world, as we know it. When the autumn, which is the harvest season, arrives, the brown leaves are gathered up and burned. What then remains? The Word of Our God--and those who receive it-- shall stand forever.

Perhaps the chief reason that the empires of this world were so prone to destruction, despite size and grandeur, is because:

a) the foundations were weak;
b) the materials were cheap.

No, it was not the lack of earthly treasures that bankrupted them, but the lack of true treasures stored in heaven (Matthew 6:19-21). Likewise, a good foundation is found by hearing and doing the words of Jesus (Matthew 7:24), so that one's life is built upon a rock. No wind, no wave, no flood can ever dislodge such a life, because it is established on a sure foundation.

History has known many shakings. The rise of Egypt, Babylon, Assyrian, Persia, Greece, and Rome all brought tremors to the world stage. The birth of Judaism, Christianity, and Islam has also left a big imprint. But what makes our time special is that the shaking is frequent, intense, global, and heavenly. Ideologies, kingdoms, and empires that have long existed have vanished without a trace. People groups who have lived in a certain territory for millennia are expelled with little warning. Moral and ethical standards that were once the bedrock of Western Civilization have been attacked mercilessly in order to reinvent things like the family, nation-state, enlightenment freedoms, and so on.

Shaking In Motion: A Walk Through History

Let us take a brief journey through modern history. At the turn of the twentieth century, the western world—which ruled most of the world—was coming out of the Victorian and Edwardian eras. Relative peace, prosperity, and technological know-how were on the increase. This first phase of globalization already began in the mid-nineteenth century, only to be halted after the First World War. The pause button would remain depressed until 1989, when the Berlin Wall collapsed. Globalization would begin anew.

During this period, secular humanism, liberal theology, neo-orthodoxy, evolution, and Marxism were coming of age, causing humanity to become disengaged from Biblical truth, long the bedrock of the western society.

> *Unlike the smooth transfer of power in a liberal democracy, the kingdoms of this world will furiously resist the advent of the Kingdom of Christ. They will have to be ejected forcibly.*

Thus detached, western society became welded to that which is material and temporal. The relative affluence and flirtation with non-Biblical ideas cause world leaders to become arrogant, self-sufficient, and independent from God.

An excellent symbol of this collision with the kingdoms of this world and the universal shaking was previously mentioned cruise ship RMS Titanic, the greatest ocean liner of its day. Standing eleven stories high and four city blocks long, it had sixteen watertight compartments. It also represented society in miniature, with first class passengers enjoying palatial suites, exquisite chandeliers, and bone china, plush carpets and decks with French cafés on them (thus eliminating space that could have been used for more much needed lifeboats). At the bottom was the steerage, where poor Irish peasants and others were searching for a new life in the New World. There were only enough lifeboats to cover half the 2,200 passengers, in part because it was believed that the ship was "unsinkable." In fact, one man bellowed "even God Himself could not sink this ship." And why have so many lifeboats when the Titanic was one big lifeboat itself?

Though the ship had the most advanced technology of its day, a very experienced crew, and was meant to sail many trips for many years, it never made it through even one journey. On Sunday night, 14 April 1912, the Titanic struck an iceberg on its maiden voyage from Southampton to New York and sunk in less than three hours. Over 1,500 passengers met a cold and icy death. Only 700 made it to the lifeboats and were saved.

The universal shaking had begun; a shot rung across the bow. Like the defiant builders of the Tower of Babel, God decided to show the people of the twentieth century that they were neither in control nor the masters of their destiny. As one survivor of the Titanic said, the tragedy "made the world rub its eyes and awake." The sound slumber was about to be interrupted forcefully.

Two years after this maritime disaster, Archduke Francis Ferndinand, heir of the Austro-Hungarian Empire, was assassinated in Sarajevo, Bosnia, on 28 June 1914. In any other time, this would have remained a local or regional issue. But this was unlike any other time--it was the time of the great shaking. This unfortunate event caused a chain reaction, which ignited the First World War, drawing combatants from far away places like India, South Africa, the United States, Australia, and New Zealand. The famous ANZAC invasion of the Gallipoli Peninsula on 25 April 1915 has forever become etched in the collective identity and memory of Australians and New Zealanders.

By the time this devastating war concluded, with the loss of millions of lives—including 60,000 soldiers from the Commonwealth of Australia—the world as it had been known had changed forever. Empires that had existed for centuries and even millennia disappeared overnight.

Ponder this massive collapse of imperial dominoes. The Chinese dynasty empire with its Emperor—gone (this was in 1911, just before the Titanic sunk). The Austro-Hungarian Empire—gone. The German Reich and its Kaiser—gone. The Russian Empire and its Tsar—gone and brutally murdered. The Ottoman Empire and its Sultan—gone. Morality and ethics also took a beating during this time, so that standards were now being openly challenged with minimal censure.

Many aftershocks would follow this global earthquake. Soon after the end of the First World War, the Spanish flu pandemic broke out in the winter of 1918-1919 with anywhere from 20 to 40 million deaths. This was followed by the "Roaring Twenties," the Great Depression, and then the Second World War. This conflict was merely the continuation of the first, but the difference was that the death toll was much higher.

Zionism, the ideology that espoused a homeland for the Jewish people in Palestine, was given a major boost by the patronage of the British Empire, courtesy of the 1917 Balfour Declaration. This would be the bedrock document of what became the British Mandate in Palestine. The

Nazis, among other atrocities, sought to implement a "Final Solution to the Jewish Problem" through the brutal extermination of European Jewry, of which two-thirds died. The Nazi Holocaust became, unwittingly, the birth pangs of the coming State of Israel in 1948.

By the end of the Second World War, we had a totally different world from that which was known when the Titanic sunk. The British Empire was crumbling, nation-states were replacing imperial rule, and communism had seized Eastern Europe and threatened to spread elsewhere in the world. The Cold War had commenced, bisecting our world into two strong and mutually antagonistic entities, both which had the nuclear firepower to destroy the other. While neither the Soviet or American superpowers ever faced each other on the battlefield during the Cold War, there were many proxy wars during this period, with both superpowers being dragged in at one time or another.

After the Cold War ended in 1989, we entered into a "New World Order," to use the phrase of US President George H.W. Bush. Yet the promised peace and prosperity tarried. Instead, Iraq under Saddam Hussein brutally invaded the nation of Kuwait in August 1990. This oil-rich nation, which had broad avenues, exquisite merchandise, a dreamy turquoise port, a Mercedes glut, tax free living with $100 billion invested for the future. Yet this ritzy civilization in the sand was turned upside down within twelve hours. The wealthy Kuwaitis either endured a ruthless occupation or became penniless refugees on the other side of the Saudi border.

Though America led a successful coalition victory to liberate Kuwait in Operation Desert Storm in January and February 1991, the shaking did not cease. The Balkans erupted into warfare while Rwanda was rent asunder by mindless genocide. Ten years after Desert Storm, al Qaeda successfully slammed hijacked airliners into the Twin Towers of New York's World Trade Center as well as the Pentagon, thus ushering a long protracted "War on Terror."

Two things are for sure: the shaking will only continue and God is in control.

Other Telltale Signs

Some other signs to look for in the coming days include the shrinkage of time (Matthew 24:22), intensity of living (Luke 17:26), worship of evil (Matthew 24:15), a falling away (II Thessalonians 2:3), celebrity culture or magnification of personality even above principles (II Thessalonians 2:4); hardening of hearts (Rev. 9:20), the collapse of character (II Timothy 3:3), and the decline of principles (I Corinthians 6:9-11). All these represent part of the great universal shaking which will lead to Alpha and Omega, the beginning of the End. Messiah's feet are at the door (James 5:9).

> *Two things are for sure: the shaking will continue and God is in control.*

REVIEW QUESTIONS:

1. What possible implication does globalization have with Bible prophecy?
2. What does *Apokatastasis* mean?
3. What parties are interested in Jerusalem, in fulfillment of Zechariah?
4. What are the two pitfalls to be avoided?
5. What two Scriptures describe the universal shaking?

Chapter Three

Interpretation: Unscrambling the Prophetic Egg

It's taken me all my life to understand that it is not necessary to understand everything —Rene-Jules-Gustave Coty (1882-1962)

The Apostle Peter rightly calls prophecy a *"light that shines in a dark place"* (II Peter 1:19). In the midst of our change-filled, crisis-riddled world, this is very reassuring. In fact, Bible prophecy could very well be your best guide for the present and future.

Yet, the fact is, there are various theories about major prophetic themes that sincerely seek to understand God's prophetic word. Some of these theories can be radically different from each other. For example, one theory says Jesus Christ will rapture the Church before the Great Tribulation, another says after. One school teaches there will be a thousand year reign of Christ on earth, while another says "no." Two millennial theories both deny a literal 1,000 year reign, but one says things on earth will get better before Christ returns while the other does not.

Why are there all these different theories? A major reason has to do with the method of interpretation. All theories interpret literally and all theories interpret symbolically—yet it is the degree of literalness versus symbolism that will separate them. Interpretation can also be influenced by the times in which we live. For example, Jewish flavoured prophetic schools have been greatly boosted by the 1948 birth of a modern Jewish state in Palestine.

Max Anders uses the term "valid uncertainties" to explain why there are various schools of thought. These uncertainties are like puzzle pieces that are missing from the picture. It is gloriously possible to see and understand the picture, but these missing pieces mean there are some details we just cannot know for sure. As such, it is unwise to be dogmatic.

Anders goes on to say that if you do not accept the notion of valid uncertainties, you will make one of two errors:

1. Fanatics: I am right and everyone else is wrong. Some people are so rigid that they even draw lines of fellowship, excluding people who believe a different eschatological theory than themselves or even implying that the other group does not even have salvation because they belong to opposite eschatological theory! OR

2. Apathetic: It is impossible for me to understand Bible prophecy[1]

Let us remember that while there are differences in interpretation of prophetic theories, some things are held in common by all legitimate parties:

1. Jesus Christ, Son of God, is Saviour and Lord;

2. The Bible is the Word of God;

3. Jesus Christ is coming back again; (Titus 2:13; 1 Peter 1:3; 3:15; 1 John 3:2-3; etc.)

---

[1] Max Anders, *What You Need to Know About Bible Prophecy in 12 Lessons*, Nashville: Thomas Nelson Publishers, 1997, page 34.

4. When Jesus returns, we will be with Him forever.

To this, we can all heartily agree and say "Amen!"

SCHOOLS OF INTERPRETATION

First of all, make a commitment to learn and understand God's Prophetic Word. We already learned that they are many benefits for the student of prophecy. The Book of Revelation even gives you a written guarantee that you will be "blessed" when you read and heed what is written (1:3).

Second, do not be insecure, flustered, or contemptuous, that there are various schools of interpretation. Have a Godly "kingdom attitude" that you will respect those who believe in a different way to you.

Regarding schools of interpretation, let us take a look at the four main ways of viewing the Book of Revelation. Bear in mind that sincere and scholarly believers belong to all these schools. Each has its own strong points and weak points. There can be areas of overlap between the schools but ultimately each is distinct from the other.

The key question that the four schools seek to answer is:

When will prophecy and the Book of Revelation be fulfilled **in the future?**

OR when was prophecy and the Book of Revelation fulfilled in **history?**

Preterism

This school of interpretation says that Revelation was already fulfilled in history, mostly in the first century A.D. It comes from the Latin word praeterire, which means "to go by" or "to pass by." A.D. 70 and the fall of Jerusalem and national Israel are considered a fulfilment of the Olivet Discourse (Matthew 24) and of other prophecies. The "666" of Revelation refers to the Roman Emperor Nero, "harlot of Babylon" who was drunk on the blood of the saints is the City of Rome, and the seven kings of Revelation 17 are seven Roman emperors. The seal, trumpet, and bowl judgements occurred in the first decades or centuries of church history. The seven letters to seven churches in Asia Minor (chapters 2 and 3) are for those churches alone.

Within preterism, there are three types, including:

1. <u>Mild Preterism:</u> Fulfillment of prophecy occurred within the first three centuries of church history. The first half of Revelation was fulfilled in A.D. 70, when Israel, considered as an enemy of the Church, was defeated. The second half was fulfilled when the Roman Emperor Constantine converted to Christianity and the church triumphed over heathen Rome in the fourth century.

2. <u>Moderate Preterism:</u> They say that most of the events of Revelation were fulfilled in history, but believe in a future Second Coming, according to Acts 1:9-11; I Corinthians 15:51-53; I Thessalonians 4:16-17.

3. Extreme Preterism: These believe that all Bible prophecy was
    fulfilled in A.D. 70 and there is nothing reserved for the future.
    This means, of course, that they reject a future Second Coming
    of Christ and bodily resurrection. Such a position is more than
    extreme—it is heresy.

On the positive side, preterism views prophecy from the writer's point of
view, which is always a good starting point in hermeneutics. However,
what value does this interpretation have for future generations, since all
(or most) of the prophecies have been fulfilled? Essentially all prophecy
is reduced to history, while major events like the Second Coming are
unfulfilled.

Historicism

To the question, when was Revelation fulfilled in history, the Historicist
says between the First Coming and Second Coming of Christ. Like
the preterist, he or she believes the prophetic fulfillment of chapters 4
through19 began in the first century (this includes the Olivet Discourse)
but it continues to be fulfilled through all of church history. Even the
letters to the seven churches are spread out like an accordion throughout
the church age, each church representing a different era of history.

For example, the first church at Ephesus corresponds to the apostolic
church of the first century, whereas the seventh and last church, Laodicea,
applies to the liberal/apostate church of today. The various "trumpet
judgements" are different historical invasions, like the Goths, Vandals,
Huns, Arabs, Turks and communists. Historicism does not hesitate to

compare the Papacy and Vatican to the antichrist, thus it is a belief of hard-core Protestantism. Indeed, it was the dominant view from the time of the Protestant Reformers until a century ago, and is still held by groups like the Mormons, Jehovah's Witnesses, and Seventh-Day Adventists, though in the main it is not as universally taught today as the other views.

The key to understanding historicist thinking is the "a day for each year" theory. The 1,260 days means 1,260 years or the seven "times" for Israel's punishment in Leviticus 26:28 becomes 2,520 years (ending around 1940, just a few years before Israel becomes a nation-state). Positively, historicism seeks to make prophetic passages relevant for every era. But Dr. Barry Chant offers these interesting comments:

> ...it seems unlikely to me that God would inspire a form of prophecy that depends so heavily on historical knowledge for its understanding. If this were the case, then the book would be basically meaningless to first century Christians, who could not possibly have the requisite historical knowledge, and to people of any subsequent century who were not students of history.[2]

Idealism

The fulfillment of prophecy and the Book of Revelation is not pegged to any particular time in history, but deals with God's principles throughout all of history. Antichrist is not just limited to Nero: he can be a Roman pope, a German Fuerher, a Soviet dictator, an Iranian ayatollah, or an al Qaeda operative, yet in the end, good wins out over evil. Idealism refers to timeless fulfillment of God's excellent ways. It can be relevant to all

---

[2] Barry Chant & Winkie Pratney, *The Return*, Chichester UK: Sovereign World, 1991, page 122.

ages and remains "principle-centered," and because it is not historically linked, people can learn the moral of the story without any historical background. However, its refusal to take a literal approach with prophetic interpretation when people, places, and times are specifically mentioned, can be a concern.

With this view, when, if ever, does history end and Christ return? Traditionally, theological liberals have favored this view with its flexible interpretation. According to Chant, however, it is becoming increasingly popular with "scholarly evangelical circles."[3] Unger accuses this view of basically ignoring the prophetic aspects of Scripture altogether.

Futurism

This view says the events of Revelation 4:1 and onwards are in the future. Like the historicists, futurists believe the seven letters to seven churches (chapters 2-3) can be applied throughout all of church history. It is, by far, the most literal interpretation of any of the views presented. The Book of Daniel and Revelation are closely tied together. History will culminate victoriously when Jesus Christ returns to earth. Within futurism are various rapture theories, like pre-tribulation, mid-tribulation, and post-tribulation. The church age is viewed as a big "parenthesis" within the prophetic calendar, which mostly applies to Israel. Futurism is popular with Evangelical and Pentecostal Christians, but not so much with the scholarly community. It has great supporters among writers like Hal Lindsey and Chuck Missler.

---

[3] Ibid, page 127.

When Is Revelation Fulfilled in History				
1st Century	Byzantine	Middle Ages	Reformation	21st Century
	Preterism			
Historicism				
Idealism				
Futurism				(21st Century or later)

The Tribulation	
Preterist	Fall of Jerusalem in A.D. 70 is the centrepiece (Luke 21:20-24)
Historicist	Tribulation reigns between the two advents of Christ (John 16:33; II Timothy 3:12)
Idealist	Tribulation always exists, only the degrees vary (Jn 16:33; Rev. 1:9; 2 Tim 3:12)
Futurist	A short, intense, and horrifying period of trouble at the end of the age (Revelation 7:14; 13:5)

The Antichrist	
Preterist	Nero or a resurrected Nero (Revelation 13:12)
Historicist	The Vatican & Papacy take the place of Christ (2 Thessalonians 2:4b)
Idealist	Antichrists will exist throughout the church age (I John 2:18-23)
Futurist	A formidable, frightening end-time leader (Revelation 13:5-17)

Henry Morris, author of *The Revelation Record*, says, "Revelation is not difficult to understand. It is difficult to believe. If you will believe it, you will understand it." [4]

---

[4] David Reagan, *The Master Plan*, Eugene OR: Harvest House Publishers, 1993, page 44.

Methods of Interpretation

It is vital that we understand how to rightly interpret Scripture, particularly prophetic passages. One of the major reasons why first-century Israel missed the First Coming of the Messiah had to do with hermeneutics; they neither understood the Scriptures nor the power of God (Mark 12:24).[5] The differences between premillennialism and amillennialism are also based on hermeneutics. Dr. Charles Feinberg made these comments:

> It can be shown that the reason the early Church was premillennial was traceable to its interpretation of the Word in a literal manner, whereas the cause of the departure from this view in later centuries of the history of the Church is directly attributable to a change in method of interpretation beginning with Origen in particular.[6]

Prophetic revelation comes in several forms, and these have to be borne in mind when practicing correct hermeneutics: parables, dreams, types, visions, ecstasies, and symbols. The latter can come in the form of events, actions, offices, institutions, persons, and/or things. With these points, let's look at the two main methods of interpretation.

---

[5] Consider the possibility of some prophetic passages compressing time. This means that a prophetic event appears to have an immediate sequence but imbedded in the prophecy is a gap of time. For example, Zechariah 9 says the King is coming, riding on donkey, and will reign over all nations. Because OT rabbis could not see gaps between first and second comings, they thought there were two messiahs, the suffering Son of Joseph and the reigning conquering Son of David. The New Testament teaches there is one Messiah who comes two times.

[6] Dwight Pentecost, *Things to Come*, Grand Rapids: Zondervan, 1958, page 2.

Allegorical Method

Allegorism is a method of interpretation where the literal meaning is merely a means of conveying a deeper and more profound spiritual meaning. Anytime the text is used to convey a figurative or moral interpretation it is also considered allegorical.

Literal Method

This is where every word is given the exact same meaning as it would have in normal everyday life. Ramm describes the literal method this way:

> The "literal" meaning of a word is the basic, customary, social designation of that word. The spiritual, or mystical meaning of a word or expression is one that arises after the literal designation and is dependent upon it for its existence.

> To interpret literally means nothing more or less than to interpret in terms of normal, usual, designation. When the manuscript alters its designation the interpreter immediately shifts his method of interpreting.[7]

This is also called the historical-grammatical method, so called because the plain meaning is measured against history and grammar. Other factors to consider include geographical, archaeological, etymological, and theological. David Cooper says:

---

[7] Bernard Ramm, Protestant Biblical Interpretation, page 64, as found in Pentecost, ibid, page 9.

When the plain sense of Scripture makes common sense, seek no other sense; therefore, take every word at its primary, ordinary, usual, literal meaning unless the facts of the immediate context studied in the light of related passages and axiomatic and fundamental truths, indicate clearly otherwise.[8]

> *Be aware that your hermeneutics can be influenced by the events and spirit of your times; so that is why a knowledge of history, grammar, and the panorama of prophecy are essential in keeping you from being "time-bound."*

A Brief History of Interpretation

Ezra the Scribe, considered the "Father of Judaism," helped reconstitute the national and religious life of Israel after the Babylonian captivity, when there was no king in Israel and the rebuilt Temple was a humbler structure than the Solomonic version. From his day and through the time of Christ and the apostles, the historical-grammatical method of interpretation was used. This is very clear in the New Testament. Christ often employed the phrase, "it is written" and spoke of the events of the Old Testament as historical fact. Early church fathers also used this method as well.

Origen began to bring a change. He tried to harmonize Scripture with Platonic philosophy and turned it into a system of interpretation. Augustine inherited Origen's allegorical interpretation. He fashioned allegorical teaching into a system of theology that dominated the church world for a millennium.

---

[8] Pentecost, ibid, page 42.

This new system of interpretation radically changed the way the church perceived issues like the Jews and Bible prophecy. For example, prophecies and promises directed to Israel were now expropriated by the Church, whereas the "curses" remained with Israel.

Such interpretation helped to kick start the very sad chapter of church-based anti-Semitism, since (Hellenized) Christendom understood that God was clearly finished with the Jews, known also as the "Christ-killers." Their disobedience had caused the abrogation of all the theocratic covenants. The only reason God had not wiped the Jews off the face of the earth was simply to preserve them as a sign of divine displeasure, and serve a warning to others. This attitude exists to this day, though it may not be so blatantly stated.

The Reformation was born when Martin Luther returned to the literal grammatical-historical method of interpretation and John Calvin systematized it. Luther actually said that every word of Scripture should be allowed to stand in its natural meaning unless faith forces us to do otherwise. This method was applied to all of Scripture **except** for prophecy; here Luther and the other Reformers continued in the tradition of Augustine. In fairness, the reformers were concerned about the doctrine of salvation (soteriology) and hence the use of literal interpretation caused a powerful tidal wave that is still felt to this day; eschatology was simply not their main focus.

Today, interpretation comes in various forms. Liberal schools use what they call "historical criticism" which implies that prophecy is simply dressed up history. It denies the literal interpretation of most anything that is prophetic and even that which is historical (e.g. the sixth century B.C. composition of the Book of Daniel, the Virgin Birth and resurrection of Christ).

Liberals and even some conservatives take a spiritualized or allegorized approach to prophetic interpretation. Conservatives, of course, believe that the Bible is the Word of God and contains supernatural revelation about the future. They interpret the non-prophetic passages in a literal manner. Even the First Coming passages are viewed literally. But with the Second Coming and the events surrounding it like the Tribulation, Millennium, and New Jerusalem, they "spiritualize" their interpretation. One needs to consider the following: if you interpret the First Coming of Christ scriptures literally, then in order to be consistent, shouldn't you do the same with Second Coming scriptures?

Rules of Interpretation

1. **Historical-Grammatical:** Interpret in the normal, historical, grammatical, and literary context. David Reagan's creed for interpretation, "I decided that if the plain sense makes sense, I would look for no other sense, lest I end up with nonsense." [9]

2. **Symbols:** When you encounter language that is clearly symbolic, look for the literal meaning behind the symbol. Sometimes Scripture gives you the meaning immediately, at other times you have to look at the whole context of Scripture for the answer. Symbols are powerful because they can paint a picture in people's minds, but misinterpretation can be highly problematic.

3. **Christ the Centrepiece:** Revelation 19:10 says that the testimony of Jesus is the spirit of prophecy. Ultimately, all prophecy is about

---

[9] Reagan, op.cit, page 43.

Jesus Christ and therefore your interpretation must be "Christological." To do otherwise is to truly miss the mark.

4. **Context:** Take notice of grammar, perspective, and harmony. Note time relationships and perspective. The original Hebrew and Greek can have subtle meanings that are important in understanding prophecy. Prophecy should be interpreted according to the neighbouring passages as well as the whole context of Scripture.

5. **Does prophecy refer to one event or more in history?** Some prophecies have an immediate and future fulfilment. Some examples include Zechariah 9:9-10:

> *9 Rejoice greatly, O daughter of Zion!*
> *Shout, O daughter of Jerusalem!*
> *Behold, your King is coming to you;*
> *He is just and having salvation,*
> *Lowly and riding on a donkey,*
> *A colt, the foal of a donkey.*
> *10 I will cut off the chariot from Ephraim*
> *And the horse from Jerusalem;*
> *The battle bow shall be cut off.*
> *He shall speak peace to the nations;*
> *His dominion shall be 'from sea to sea,*
> *And from the River to the ends of the earth.*

Verse 9 is clearly about the First Coming of Christ while Verse 10 is about the Second. In Isaiah 11:1-5 the first two verses are about the First Coming and the rest are the Second. In the Nazareth synagogue Jesus read Isaiah 61:1-2 all the way to "to proclaim the acceptable year of the Lord" and then he stopped. He declared that "This day is this scripture fulfilled in your ears," thus giving this passage a First Coming fulfilment. However, He deliberately omitted the following phrase, "...*the day of vengeance of our God*" which clearly fits the Second Coming (II Thessalonians 1:8).

THREE KEY ISSUES
FOR ESCHATOLOGICAL HERMENEUTICS
(ALSO CALLED THE THREE "I's")

Three issues need to be considered when you undertake the hermeneutics of Bible prophecy. Your answers to the following questions will cause you to take a certain eschatological stance. It is almost impossible to come up with something new or different, because all the main options have been broached over the past two thousand years.

1. **Interpretation:** How literal or allegorical will you take each passage of Scripture? While all Bible students will employ both, it is the degree to which they apply it that will determine the eschatological school to which they will eventually belong.

2. **Imminence:** Can Christ return anytime He wants or must certain signs be fulfilled first before He can appear? Your answer to this simple question will definitely assign you to a long-held position.

3. **Israel:** Does Israel have an end-time destiny or not? Is there a difference between the Jew, Gentile, and the Church? Is God finished with the Jews? Does He have one chosen people or two? Again, your eschatological position will be determined by your attitude to the Jews and Israel.

REVIEW QUESTIONS:

1. Name the four schools of interpretation.
2. What are the two methods of interpretation?
3. Which method of interpretation did Ezra, Christ, the Apostles, and the early church use?
4. Who pioneered the allegorical system?
5. What method was used by the Protestant Reformers?

Part Two

A Sure Foundation

Chapter Four

A Sure Foundation Part I: The Covenants

Jacob the Patriarch had spent twenty years in Padan Aram, where he was transformed from a penniless bachelor into a man of great wealth, married with children. Now it was time to go home to Canaan. The journey was tough: the entourage travelled slowly and he was being harassed with uncle Laban on his back and brother Esau in his face. He wanted to go forward with his life, but how? The Word of the Lord to him was simple: arise and go back to Bethel (Genesis 35:1).

The Bible has several ironies, which is God's way of showing that He does things differently to people. His thoughts and ways are always higher than ours. We learn that:

- If you want to receive, learn to be a give.
- If you want to have friends, learn to be friendly.
- If you want to be exalted, learn to be humble.
- If you want to be first, learn to be last.
- If you want to save your life, learn to lose it for the cause of Christ.

Now we are about to learn a new irony from the Lord: if you want to go forward, then go back!

Bethel, which means "house of God," was the very place Jacob sojourned on his way to Padam Aram when he was fleeing from his brother Esau (Genesis 28). Though he was not in a strong spiritual state, he had his first recorded experience with the presence of God. In some ways, the Bethel visit was Jacob's "conversion experience." Here he covenanted with God to give Him tithes of all if He would bring Jacob back safely to the land of promise.

So now twenty years later God commands him to return to Bethel, as the beginning of the next phase of his life; to come back to the place where he first met with God. Bethel, the house of God, is where you receive your "first love" and do the "first works." These things are so important that Christ commanded the Ephesian church to return to these "first" or else risk losing their candlestick from its place (Revelation 2:4-5). Where can you obtain these things again? Back at Bethel! Bethel is where we begin our walk with God and Bethel is where you return to in order to go forward.

> *One of God's great ironies: if you want to go forward with your life and destiny, learn to go back to Bethel, the place where you first met God.*

If we want to understand the future, we need to know the past. When it comes to Biblical eschatology, then it is fundamental that we understand the theocratic covenants of the Bible. Without this, it is impossible to have a clear understanding. Dwight Pentecost puts it this way:

> The covenants contained in the Scriptures are of primary importance to the interpreter of the Word and to the student of Eschatology. God's eschatological program is determined and prescribed by these

covenants and one's eschatological system is determined and limited by the interpretation of them. These covenants must be studied diligently as the basis of Biblical Eschatology.[1]

> *Unfulfilled covenantal promises will take place in the future, thus making them part of Biblical eschatology. God's faithful character will allow no other conclusion.*

To give you a simple clue: if God made an unconditional promise through a Biblical covenant, it has not yet been fulfilled, and we know that God's promises are immutable and His character sure, then the promise will have its fulfilment in the future. It becomes part of the doctrine of last things.

Covenant Defined

Covenant is not part of our daily vocabulary. From a western point-of-view, covenant may seem to be an antiquated practice with no relevance for today. The closest analogy we have to covenant in the West is marriage, and even that parallel has its problems. Like covenant, marriage is meant to be permanent, but with the dissolution of marriage rising to an all-time high, one wonders whether it is possible to understand this important doctrine.

The answer is "yes." We can understand. Here is why.

The word "covenant" comes from the Hebrew word *brit* and the Greek word *diatheke*, which means a strong and binding agreement between

---

[1] Dwight Pentecost, Things to Come, Grand Rapids: Zondervan, 1964, page 65.

two parties. It can be between two individuals, two peoples, or between an individual or group thereof and God Himself. It is when two parties voluntarily enter into an agreement to do something for the other party.

When the terms and conditions are met, there is great blessing. If broken, the consequences can be disastrous (e.g. not unlike a "divorce," which is the breaking of the marriage vows). In some cases, there may be no conditions at all; the second party becomes the inevitable beneficiary of the first party, without any effort on their part.

Fundamentally, Christians should be able to relate to covenants because our Bible is made up of two covenants: an old covenant or Old Testament and a new covenant or the New Testament.

Three types of covenants were found in the ancient Middle East:

The first was called "parity," which was made between two equals in order to cooperate or respect the others. Examples of these include Abraham and Abimelech (Genesis 21:27) as well as Jonathan and David (I Samuel 18:1-4 and II Samuel 9:1-13).

The second was called Suzerain to Vassal, where a great power entered into covenant with a minor power. The "superpower" demands tribute, service and loyalty from the vassal and in return the vassal receives superpower patronage. Judah had contemplated such an arrangement with Egypt, to the consternation of the prophet Isaiah. Chedorlaomer in Genesis 14 was one example and, for that matter, so was the Mosaic covenant, made between God and Moses in Deuteronomy. This type of covenant was clearly conditional and if dishonoured, the Suzerain would greatly punish the vassal.

The third example was simply called the Royal Grant. The King would give an inheritance to a faithful subject, usually land or something else of value, and the descendents of the subject would also retain the inheritance if they remained loyal to the monarch. This type of covenant was considered unconditional. Examples include 1 Samuel 8:14; 22:7; 27:6; Esther 8:1.

In the Bible, we have eight theocratic covenants mentioned. There are, in order of occurrence:

1. Edenic (Genesis 1:28-30; 2:15-17)
2. Adamic (Genesis 3:14-19)
3. Noahic (Genesis 8:20-9:17)
4. Abrahamic (Genesis 12:1-3)
5. Mosaic (Exodus 20-23; Deuteronomy)
6. Palestinian (Deuteronomy 30:1-10)
7. Davidic (2 Samuel 7:4-17)
8. New (Jeremiah 31:31-37)

Though most of these covenants were initially made between God and an individual, they had ramifications for the heirs, successors, and/or chosen people. For the purposes of eschatology, we will explore covenants 4-8.

Conditional or Unconditional?

When it comes to the theocratic covenants, it is of the utmost importance to determine whether the covenant is conditional or unconditional. For example, if God promises to give Israel the borders between the "river of Egypt and the river Euphrates," and it has not yet happened, then it **will** happen in the future because of God's unblemished character. If, on the other hand, the promise is conditional on Israel's obedience, then due to its great rebellion God is no longer obligated to fulfil it.

Conditional: Fulfilment of the covenantal promise is dependent on the obedience of the recipient (e.g. Israel). Disobedience renders the promise null and void. "If you will" becomes the dominant phrase.

Unconditional: Fulfilment of the covenantal promise has little to do with the recipient and **everything** to do with the benefactor, namely God. He will deliver His promise, no matter what, but it will be on His terms, in His own way and His own timing. "I will" is the key statement.

Arnold Fruchtenbaum says this about unconditional covenants:

> An unconditional covenant can be defined as a sovereign act of God whereby God unconditionally obligates Himself to bring to pass definite promises, blessings, and conditions for the covenanted people. It is a unilateral covenant. This type of covenant is characterized by the formula "I will," which declares God's determination to do exactly as He promised. The blessings are secured by the grace of God.[2]

You are urged to study the covenants for yourself and, as good Berean Christians, search the scripture daily to see if these things are so (Acts 17:11).

Abrahamic Covenant

Reference: Genesis 12:1-3, 7; 13:14-17; 15:1-21; 17:1-21; 22:15-18.

---

[2] Arnold Fruchtenbaum, Israelology: *The Missing Link in Systematic Theology*, Tustin CA: Ariel Ministries 1993, page 570.

Described as the "mother of all theocratic covenants," this foundational agreement between God and Abraham has ramifications that are still felt to this day.

God made some incredible promises to Abraham. From every angle it appears to be unconditional. This is marked by the phrase "I will." In essence, this covenant can be summarized under three main "I will" clauses:

1. **Land:** *"Get out of your country ... to the land that **I will** show you"* God is promising to give to Abraham and his descendents the land of Canaan (12:1, 5-7; 13:14, 15, 17; 15:18-21; 17:8). This will be amplified in the Palestinian covenant.

2. **Seed:** *"**I will** make you a great nation"* (12:2, also 13:16; 15:5; 17:1, 2, 7; 22:17). Up to this point, the man's name was merely Abram, which means "exalted father." This is ironic because up until now he had no children. Now God is promising that the "exalted father" will actually become a father—of many nations, which is the meaning of his new name, Abraham. Considering Abraham's advanced age and the crowded conditions in his inheritance, Canaan, he would need a miracle of God to have this provision fulfilled, as indeed for all three provisions. The "seed" aspect is amplified in the Davidic Covenant.

3. **Blessing:** *"**I will** bless those who bless you, and I will curse him who curses you; and in you all the families of the earth shall be blessed"* (12:3; 22:18). Eventually Abraham would become the father of Israel but the blessing would be spread to all peoples and nations. This finds fulfilment in the New Covenant.

Abraham is the great Old Testament prototype of two wonderful goals to which every believer should aspire: a man of faith and the friend of God. If you want to grow in these areas, a study of Abraham's life in the Bible is in order. God truly did give him a son, Isaac, but it is the later son Jesus by which all the nations of the earth have been blessed.

Paul speaks of the Abrahamic covenant in Galatians 3:16-17 (NKJV):

Now to Abraham and his Seed were the promises made. He does not say, "and to seeds," as of many, but as of one, "And to your Seed," who is Christ. 17 And this I say, that the law, which was four hundred and thirty years later, cannot annul the covenant that was confirmed before by God in Christ, that it should make the promise of none effect.

As the Apostle to the Gentiles, Paul assures them that the blessings of Abraham belong to all the nations of the earth, because Abraham's seed, namely Jesus Christ, is the conduit of that blessing. All people of faith, from any nation, find the spiritual blessing of the Abrahamic covenant in Christ. It is foundational for all spiritual life because it predates the Mosaic covenant by 430 years and the seed is Christ. He affirms that if you belong to Christ, you are Abraham's seed and heirs according to the promise (Galatians 3:29).

Though the Bible clearly defines spiritual blessing through Abraham, will there also be literal, material fulfilment? Will there also be a land given to the natural seed of Abraham? To this question, we must ask the question. "Did the natural seed of Abraham, Israel, inherit the land of Canaan in history?" The answer should be clear.

If there is a literal and eternal fulfilment of this unconditional covenant, then it will have major repercussions in the latter days.

Mosaic Covenant

Reference: Exodus 20:1-Deuternomy 28:68

Mosaic covenant laid down the basis of fellowship with God. Originally given in Exodus and amplified in Deuteronomy, it can be divided into three parts:

1. **Covenant & Commandments Exodus 20:1-26:** Ten Commandments that govern the person's life with God and others. Here the covenant is revealed.

2. **Judgements and the Tabernacle Exodus 21:1-23:33:** Case studies where specific situations and solutions are given.

3. **Priests and Ordinances Exodus 24:12 – 31:18:** directs how to live the religious life before God

The centrepiece of the covenant was the blood sacrifice found in Leviticus 17:11:

For the life of the flesh is in the blood, and I have given it to you upon the altar to make atonement for your souls; for it is the blood that makes atonement for the soul.

Remember that the word "atonement" means to cover one's sin, but it cannot, by itself remove sin. Only the body and blood of Jesus Christ can do that (Hebrews 10:4, 10, 12, 14, 18, and 19).

A good summary of the Mosaic covenant was "Do this ... and you shall live" or "Do this ... and God shall be your God." The problem is that Israel was not able to keep the law and this brought judgement and dispersion. But Gentiles need not get conceited, because they would not be able to keep the law, either. For if you transgress one commandment or precept, it is as if you have broken them all.

The Mosaic covenant was clearly a conditional one. Exodus 19:5f says *"Now therefore,* **if you will** (NOTE: "I will") *indeed obey My voice and keep My Covenant, then you shall be a special treasure to Me..."* By virtue of the word "if" confirms its conditionality. This is further confirmed in Deuteronomy 28 where there are 13 verses of blessing **IF** you keep the commands of God and 54 verses of curses if you do not.

So if the Mosaic Covenant was conditional and if it could not cleanse from sin, then what was its purpose? Fortunately, the Lord revealed this to the Apostle Paul, who shows us with great clarity.

> *...For if there had been a law (Mosaic Covenant) given which could have given life, truly righteousness would have been by the law. Therefore the law was our tutor to bring us to Christ, that we might be justified by faith. But after faith has come, we are no longer under a tutor—Galatians 3:21, 24, 25*

The Mosaic Covenant was like a tutor and bodyguard who protected the heirs of God's grace until they reached full age (Galatians 4:4-7). The repetitive animal sacrifices and blood atonement were a prophetic foretaste of the abhorrent yet universal nature of sin and how the remission of sins required the shedding of blood (Hebrews 9:22; 10:1-4). The remarkable thing is that the high priest offered daily sacrifices and yet when it came to the Most Holy Place of God, he could only enter in once a year for a few hours. Jesus Christ offers one sacrifice and He lives there perpetually, where He makes intercession for us (Hebrews 7:25). Furthermore, because of the "once and for all" sacrifice of Christ, all believers can boldly, even daily, come to the throne of grace where they can find grace and mercy in time of need (Hebrews 4:16).

So what is the value of the Mosaic Covenant and Law to a believer in Christ today? Remember, that all Scripture is given by inspiration of God and is profitable (II Timothy 3:16) ... and that includes the Mosaic Covenant. Because "...*the law is holy, and the commandment holy and just and good*" (Romans 7:12), the Law serves as the measuring stick that reveals God's righteous principles and consequentially humanity's depraved ways (I Timothy 1:8-10).

So the law is the tutor that brings us to Christ. It is like the mirror which shows our unrighteousness and how desperately we need the Saviour. Great evangelists, especially of yesteryear, used the preaching of the Law to great effect. One evangelistic formulation is preach 90% law and 10% grace.

The Law is also an object lesson about God's righteousness and how believers cannot attain to this righteousness through their own efforts (Romans 8:2-4). Finally, the teaching of the Tabernacle (Exodus 24:12-27:21 and Hebrews 9:1-5) is a Biblically-validated "type" to illustrate the redemptive work of Christ.

> *Daily sacrifices allowed only one man to appear before God, once a year; one sacrifice of Jesus Christ allows every believer to appear before God daily and for all time.*

Moses' Covenant led to the blood sacrifice to atone for the sins of the people. The sacrifice could cover—but not remove—the sin problem and nature. When we get to the New Covenant, it will be clear whose blood ratifies this covenant.

Palestinian Covenant

Reference: Deuteronomy 29:1 – 30:10; see also Jeremiah 23:5-8; Ezekiel 20:42-44; 36:24-30; 37:11-14; 47:1-48:35; Zechariah 12:10-13:2.

Originally part of the Mosaic Covenant, it becomes a stand-alone arrangement when it is connected to the Abrahamic covenant, where it fulfils the "land" aspect. Under Moses, this covenant is conditional: keeping of the law is the pre-requisite for having victory over enemies, protection from locusts, abundant rain and plentiful harvest. But when the covenant is linked to Abraham, it becomes unconditional (Genesis 12:1; 13:14, 15) and has eschatological implications.

According to Arnold Fruchtenbaum, the following provision will happen in the Palestinian Covenant in the last days (all the references are found in the Book of Deuteronomy):

1. The nation will be plucked off the land for unfaithfulness (29:2-30:2).

2. There will be a future repentance of Israel (30:2).
3. Their Messiah will return (30:3).
4. Israel will be regathered (30:3, 4).
5. Israel will be restored to the land (30:5).
6. Israel will be converted as a nation (30:6).
7. Israel's enemies will be judged (30:7).
8. The nation will then receive her full blessing of the messianic kingdom (30:8-10).[3]

The prophets of Israel also saw a glorious future return to the land. Isaiah told of a highway through the deserts and mountains that would lead God's people back to the land in the Messianic era (49:8-13). Ezekiel saw a restored Temple and the land redistributed according to the tribes (Chapters 40 to 48). For Zechariah the exiles of Babylon came home with the hope that God would meet them in Jerusalem and set up His earthly reign (8:1-5). Judas Maccabee and his army fought and prevailed against the Seleucid Syrians in the hope that the Kingdom of God would come to earth.

Davidic Covenant

Reference: II Samuel 7:11-17; I Chronicles 17:10-15; Psalm 89:3-4; Jeremiah 33:22, 25-26

This remarkable covenant came about in a heart-warming way. King David realized that the God who had promoted, protected, and blessed him, lived in a tent (i.e. the Ark of the Covenant was housed in the tabernacle) while David himself lived in a house of cedar. This was inappropriate. Why should the servant live better than the Master? God's ark needed a house as well.

---

[3] Arnold Fruchtenbaum, Israelology: The Missing Link in Systematic Theology, Tustin CA: Ariel Ministries 1993, page 582.

After sharing his desire with Nathan, the prophet responded that David should proceed with what was planned. But soon thereafter, God said "no." David would not build the house of the Lord, later to be known as The Temple. He was a man with a lot blood on his hands due to much warfare. But God graciously offered David something far better. He would build David a house, an indestructible dynasty.

From this exchange came what has become known as the Davidic covenant. It represents the "seed" aspect of the Abrahamic covenant. Provision of the covenant is spelled out under the following terms:

1. **Permanence:** Instead of David building God a house, it would be God who makes David an "indestructible" house or dynasty (II Samuel 7:11ff; I Chronicles 17:10ff);

2. **Immediate Heir:** Solomon, who was destined to be David's heir apparent, would be established on his father's throne (II Samuel 7:12; I Chronicles 17:11);

3. **Temple:** It would be Solomon who builds The Temple (verse 13; I Chronicles 17:12);

4. **Perpetuity:** The throne of David would be established forever (verses 13ff and 16; I Chronicles 17:12).

5. **Fatherhood:** God would be the "Father" to the son of David (verse 14; I Chronicles 17:13);

6. **Chastisement:** If the son of David was disobedient, God would chasten him through other people (verse 14). Solomon was chastened for his own sins. Jesus, the greater "son of David," was chastened for the sins of humanity.

7. **Perpetual Mercy:** Even if chastened, God's mercy would not depart from the son of David (I Chronicles 17:14).

8. **Genealogy of Messiah:** Messiah will be from the House of David (I Chronicles 17:11).

9. **Everlasting Kingdom:** Messiah and His reign will be established forever (I Chronicles 17:12-14).

In essence, David would rule the people of God in the Promised Land (II Samuel 7:10), in harmony with the Palestinian covenant. The House of David would be a permanent dynasty (verses 11-16). This Godly King will provide the people of God peace and rest in the land of promise. The Kingdom established by the Son of David would endure forever (verses 13, 16; Luke 1:33).

This covenant is so important that it is confirmed by other passages like Psalm 89; Isaiah 9:6,7; 11:1; Jeremiah 23:5,6; 30:8,9; 33:14-17,19-26; Ezekiel 37:24,25; Hosea 3:4,5; Amos 9:11; Luke 1:30-35,68-70; Acts 15:14-18.

What does the Davidic covenant have to do with eschatology? If it is unconditional, then at some point the Messiah, the Son of David, will need to rule and reign from David's throne in Jerusalem. Read Isaiah 49

> *What does the Davidic covenant have to do with eschatology? If it is unconditional, then at some point the Messiah, the Son of David, will need to rule and reign from David's throne in Jerusalem.*

for more details, since the Messiah was called from His mother's womb (v. 1), will restore Israel, bring salvation to the nations (v. 6, 8), reassure Israel (v. 14) that its future will be glorious (versus 15-21) and that it will be the head nation (vs. 22-23). Clearly these things have not yet literally happened, so the final fulfilment would need to be in the future. That future time is known as the Millennium.

But Messiah is more than just the Son of David. On this point Jesus stumped the Pharisees when He asked the questions "What do you think of Christ? Whose son is he?" His brilliant response was to quote Psalm 110:1 (NKJV), which reads:

The LORD said to my Lord,
Sit at My right hand,
Till I make Your enemies Your footstool.

The Lord then asks the crucial question: If David calls the Messiah "Lord," then how can this same Messiah be David's son? They were speechless; how is He his Son (Matthew 22:45)? To say that Messiah is the Son of David only tells half the story, because He is also the Son of God. Remember that Christianity did not take the Man Christ Jesus and make Him to be God; it was the Son of God Christ Jesus who willingly became a man. We call this event the incarnation and it changed history.

The New Covenant

Reference: Jeremiah 31:31-34

Like all the previous covenants, it was made with Israel and also amplifies the Abrahamic covenant, particularly the "blessing" aspect. Prophesied to rebellious Judah at the time of its expulsion from the Promised Land, it was God's gracious way of saying that He would fulfil all that He promised. Main tenets include:

1. **New Covenant is For All Israel:** Given to the House of Israel and the House of Judah (Jeremiah 31:31);

2. **Different to Moses:** Mosaic Covenant was broken but this one will endure (Verse 32)

3. **Regeneration:** The law of God will now be on minds and hearts, not tablets of stone; all Israel shall be saved (verse 33; Isaiah 59:2; 61:9; Romans 11:25-27);

4. **Adoption:** They will become again (or renewed as) the people of God (verse 33).

5. **Indwelling Holy Spirit:** The indwelling of God's law (verse 33) is only possible by the Holy Spirit (Ezekiel 36:26-27).

6. **Universal Knowledge:** All Israel will know the Lord (verse 34).

7. **Forgiveness:** All Israel would receive forgiveness of sins (verse 34).

It is none other than Jesus Christ who ratifies the New Covenant. He says, *"For this is My Blood of the new covenant, which is shed for man for the remission of sins"* (Matthew 26:28; Zechariah 9:11; Mark 14:24; Luke 22:20; I Corinthians 11:25). In II Corinthians 3, the Apostle Paul shows that the Christian life is not based on the external and temporary Mosaic covenant, which he calls "the ministry of death and condemnation."(II Corinthians 3:7, 9).

Instead, true Christian living is founded on the New Covenant, which is called the "ministry of Spirit" and "ministry of righteousness" (II Corinthians 3:8-11). Read the Book of Hebrews if you want more insight on the New Covenant. Taken on literal interpretation, the physical aspects of the covenant are fulfilled in Israel while the spiritual side blesses the Gentiles.

If the New Covenant is unconditional, then it has profound implications for eschatology and the future. Messiah will return to earth. Israel will be protected and preserved among the nations, and restored to the Promised Land, where it will be materially blessed (Jeremiah 32:41; Isaiah 61:8; Ezekiel 34:25-27). Upon its return, Israel will be converted, regenerated, forgiven, and restored. The Messiah will personally return and supervise the salvation, forgiveness, restoration and blessing on Israel as He pours out the Holy Spirit on them. Even the land will be reclaimed and rebuilt, becoming the glorious center of the whole world. The sanctuary will be rebuilt (Ezekiel 37:26-27) and wars will be supplanted by universal peace and righteousness (Hosea 2:18; Isaiah 2:4).

> *To say that Messiah is the Son of David only tells half the story, because He is also the Son of God.*

On the assumption that the Abrahamic Covenant and its ancillary Palestinian, Davidic, and New Covenants are all unconditional, then the unfulfilled aspects of these covenants are destined to play a significant part in our future when the Lord Jesus Christ returns to earth. May the Lord hasten that day (Revelation 22:17).

REVIEW QUESTIONS:

1. Define covenant in your own words.
2. What aspects of the Abrahamic covenant were found in:
   a) The Palestinian Covenant
   b) The Davidic Covenant
   c) The New Covenant?
3. What relationship do these ancient theocratic covenants have with eschatology?
4. Who are the "two fathers" of Jesus Christ?

Chapter Five

A Sure Foundation Part II: Book of Daniel And Nebuchadnezzar's Statue

Dreams, visions, interpretations, changing empires, exile, and return: all these constitute the pillars of the magnificent book of Daniel. Without exaggeration, it is an intensely spiritual book in the midst of a corpus of literature that has been literally Spirit-inspired. A panoramic sweep of ancient history parades before the reader. It can be a full and breath-taking experience.

Yet above all else, Daniel is far more than a spiritual history book. It gives us major insights about the future. Nebuchadnezzar's Statue and the Seventy Week Prophecy become significant themes in the prophetic calendar. Without Daniel, it would be difficult, perhaps impossible, to understand major prophetic utterances like the Olivet Discourse (Matthew 24, Mark 13, Luke 21), II Thessalonians 2, and the Book of Revelation. He speaks about antichrist, the great tribulation, times of the Gentiles, the Second Coming, resurrections and judgements. We can confidently say that the Book of Daniel is the foundational book of all end-time prophecy.

A Brief Introduction

The Book of Daniel is named after its author. The Hebrew name dani'el means "God is my Judge." Born of royal seed (1:3), young Daniel is deported to Babylon along with his friends, where he is given the name

Belteshazzar "Bel Protect His Life." He is trained at the Babylonian court, where he spends much of his life. His public career includes being governor of Babylon and, even as an old man, he continues to work under the Medo-Persians. He is a contemporary of Jeremiah, Ezekiel (a fellow exile), and Zerubbabel. Daniel lives through the entire seventy year captivity of Judah to Babylon and survives long enough to see a minority of his people return to Jerusalem under Cyrus the Great.

The most significant aspect of his career was not as a civil servant for two ancient empires, but by being the man of God who could interpret visions and dreams. Nine out of twelve chapters are replete with dreams and visions that pertain to God's dealings with Israel and the nations.

The immense detail of fulfilled prophetic utterances, with chapter 11 alone having over one hundred predictions, has caused some critics to say that Daniel was written, not in the sixth century, but in the second century B.C. during the time of the Maccabees. But the case for late date Daniel is not convincing and attitudinally problematic. Not only does it imply unbelief, saying God cannot give detailed prophecy in advance, but it hints that the author of Daniel was being deceptive. God certainly was able to give hundreds of details in the first coming prophecies of Jesus. In any case, because Jesus Christ Himself vouched for the credibility and legitimacy of Daniel, so should we.

Of interest is that in the Hebrew Bible (the Old Testament) the Book of Daniel is not listed among the prophetic books. The apparent reason is that Daniel never actually makes any known or recorded prophetic utterances, though he does interpret dreams. In the Christian Bible, Daniel is placed among the major prophetical books. The reason that Christians call him a prophet is because Jesus did (Matthew 24:15). As always, Jesus' standard sets the standard. A good title would be Daniel, the Prophet from Babylon.

Historically, Babylon overcame Assyria in 612 B.C. and became the dominant empire of Mesopotamia. It then took over the Middle East in 605 B.C. with the defeat of Egypt. Shortly after this, Daniel was deported to Babylon. Seventy years later under the patronage of Cyrus the Great and the victorious Medo-Persians, Babylon is defeated (but not destroyed) and Zerubbabel leads groups of exiles back to Jerusalem. Daniel lives until the third year of Cyrus (536 B.C.). The Persian Empire lasts around two hundred years, when the Hellenistic empire of Alexander the Great supplants it. This realm lasted until the first century B.C., when Rome became masters of the region.

Nebuchadnezzar's Statue

This prophecy is found in Daniel Chapter Two. In the second year of his reign, Nebuchadnezzar is in charge of an impressive empire and imperial city, the likes of which were unrivalled in the ancient Near East. Despite his achievements, the king was extremely anxious and exceptionally irrational. A study of the Book of Daniel is worthwhile just to discover how our man dealt with difficult people; if he could survive a Nebuchadnezzar, you can learn how to overcome anyone!

One night Nebuchadnezzar had a dream but his spirit was so troubled that he could no longer sleep. He called the astrologers, sorcerers, and magicians of Babylon, known as "wise men", and demanded that they explain the dream. It was their job to give interpretations. But what the

Outline of the Book of Daniel	
Chapter	**Description**
One	Daniel Deported to Babylon; Brought to Court; Faithful in Issue of Food
Two	Nebuchadnezzar's Statue (Dream) Tells about Babylon, Persia, Greece, Rome
Three	Nebuchadnezzar's Image of Gold and Daniel's Friends in the Fiery Furnace
Four	Nebuchadnezzar's Vision of a Great Tree; His Humiliation & Restoration
Five	Belteshazzar and the Handwriting on the Wall
Six	Daniel Promoted in Persia and His Survival in the Lion's Den
Seven	Daniel's Vision of a Lion, Bear, Leopard, & Terrifying Beast; Ancient of Days
Eight	Daniel's Vision of the Ram, the Male Goat, and the Little Horn (Antichrist)
Nine	Daniel's Intercession; Gabriel Reveals to Him the Seventy Week Prophecy
Ten	Daniel's Three Week Fast and the Visit of the Heavenly Messenger
Eleven	Revelation of the Sixty-Nine Weeks (Greece & Persia) and Seventieth Week
Twelve	Prophecy of Great Time of Trouble and Resurrection; the Book Sealed

king demanded was that they also tell him what the dream was first, since he apparently forgot it. This demand was not just unreasonable; it was totally unprecedented. When the wise men of Babylon could not comply, the king hastily and angrily decreed that all of them be destroyed. This included Daniel and his friends.

The killing spree had already begun when the king's guard found Daniel. He managed to buy sufficient time from the King to consult with his three friends and then corporately seek God for the description and explanation of the king's dream. Their lives depended on it and God faithfully complied.

The Dream Described (2:31-35)

When Daniel appeared before the king, he described the dream. It basically consisted of a statue and a stone. The statue was made of multiple ingredients: a head of fine gold, arms and chest of silver, belly and thighs of bronze, legs of iron, and feet of iron and clay.

The stone was cut out of the mountain without hands. It strikes the statue at its feet and the entire edifice crumbles into a pile of dust. The wind comes and blows the dust away, like chaff from the summer threshing floor. Not a speck of dust remains. It is as if the statue never existed.

All that is now left is the stone. It begins to grow rapidly until it becomes a great mountain and fills the whole earth.

The Dream Interpreted (2:36-45)

This statue describes nothing less than the prophetic period known as the

"Times of the Gentiles," which spans the period from Daniel's day until the Second Coming of Christ. These Gentile powers will interact, and in many cases, oppress, the people of God.

Head of Gold—Babylon (612-539 B.C.) Nebuchadnezzar and his kingdom are the head of fine gold. Their kingdom, as well as legacy, was nothing short of awesome. Here is where civilization began and, prophetically and possibly literally, will culminate. Agriculture, numbering system, cosmetics, bureaucracies, city-states, and much more came out of Babylon. So did cruelty and false religion. Approximately seven chapters of Scripture are devoted to its fall (Isaiah 13, 14, 47; Jeremiah 50 and 51; Revelation 17 and 18). This many chapters involve a lot of detail, much which awaits a future fulfillment. Judging Babylon for all its sins and crimes would be consistent with the justice of God. Babylon was a religious place without God.

Arms and Chest of Silver—Medo Persia (539-331 B.C.): The Persian Empire was the successor realm to Babylon, and spanned 127 provinces from India to Ethiopia. It was known for its high level of culture, sophistication, tolerance, enlightenment, and multiculturalism. It was Persia under Cyrus the Great that gave the opportunity for Jews to return to Judah, if they so desired, and even provided support to begin the rebuilding process.

Despite this progressive and supportive mindset, it was ironically Persia— not the demanding Babylonians or war-like Assyrians--that posed the greatest existential, even mortal, threat that Israel had ever faced to date. For it was the Persian Prime Minister Haman, who decreed that all Jews in the realm should be murdered on the 9th Day of Adar. The absolute reverence for the law of the Medes and Persians, which cannot be altered

(Lex is Rex, not Rex is Lex) and the efficient infrastructure, made this ancient decree for the complete annihilation of the Jewish people totally plausible.

It was only due to the sovereignty of God by placing a courageous Jewish orphan named Esther as Queen of Persia that Haman's scheme was foiled, at the last minute. Had Esther not intervened, Biblical and Messianic history would have been abruptly terminated. Persia represents *lex* without God.

Belly and Thigh of Bronze—Greek or Hellenistic Empire (331-63 B.C.): The young and legendary Macedonian named Alexander the Great, credited for "conquering the world," in reality conquered the Persian Empire. This man had a mission: to export Greek language and culture to the world. He planted Greek colonies as far away as Afghanistan, and this included Ten Greek Cities in ancient Israel, known in the Gospels as the *Decapolis*.

The process of imparting all things Greek is known as *Hellenism*, whose influence has forged Western Civilization. Hellenism bestowed on Israel the Septuagint (LXX), which is the Greek translation of the Hebrew Old Testament and became the Bible of the Early Church. It also gave the Church its New Testament, Creeds, Church Councils, and the queen of all subjects, Theology.

Despite its positive points and beauty, Hellenism could also be extremely seductive and spiritually destabilizing. Ancient Israel was so eager to join the "Hellenic Club" that it changed its names from Hebrew to Greek, built a gymnasium in Jerusalem, and almost succeed in becoming like all the other nations.

When Antiochus IV (known also as Epiphanes, God-Manifest) offered the sacrilegious sacrifice of a swine on the high altar at the Jerusalem Temple in 168 B.C., many Israelites were so desensitized by Hellenism that they considered such an abomination neutral, if not normal.

Only the minority military revolt of Judas Maccabee, like a Phinehas of old, galvanized Israel and caused them to expel the Seleucid regime out of the country. But the successor Hasmonean dynasty found it impossible to depart from the spiritually corrupting influence of Hellenism and eventually succumbed to Rome in 63 B.C. Hellenism represents human philosophy and wisdom without God.

Legs of Iron, Feet of Iron and Clay—Imperial Empire (63 B.C. to 476 A.D. and beyond): Many Bible teachers say that this aspect of the statue represents Rome. The Roman Empire spanned southern Europe, North Africa, and the Middle East all the way to Persia. It adopted some of the best aspects of Hellenism, hence the term "Greco-Roman." Its philosophy of law, justice, and roads were the role model for ancient civilization. They allowed Israel a degree of religious and political autonomy, provided they paid their taxes and kept the peace.

Eventually Rome split into an Eastern and Western branch, run by Constantinople and Rome, respectively. This decentralization meant that there would be literally two east/west superpowers for the next sixteen hundred years. After Rome fell in A.D. 476, then the center of western power went to France, followed by Germany. After Constantinople fell in 1453 A.D., the center of eastern power went to Moscow, which has been called "The Third Rome." Of interest is that the imperial ruler of the Germans was called Kaiser, while that of the Russians was Tsar. Both of these names mean Caesar, harkening back to the Roman or Imperial underpinnings of the empire. Rome symbolizes power without God.

Eventually, the two legs of iron will merge into the feet of iron and clay, representing partial strength and partial weakness. After 1,600 years the East/West balance of power gave way to a single power, the precursor of a one-world government. During that time, the world was still in a Cold War between two rival superpowers: the United States and its (Western) European Allies of NATO versus the Soviet Union and its (Eastern) European Allies called the Warsaw Pact. With the collapse of the Soviet Union in 1991, the world has been left with a single superpower and a greatly enlarged "United Nations" which has gone far beyond its original mandate of maintaining world peace to endeavoring to administer global governance. As Fruchtenbaum says:

> ...Rome must not be seen as the total fourth empire, but only as the first stage of the Empire of Imperialism. The third stage, which will be a one world government stage, will happen at some point when the East-West division stage collapses.[1]

The Stone Cut Out of the Mountain Without Hands: This is nothing less than Jesus Christ and His Kingdom. The term "cut without hands" speaks of its non-human, or divine origin. This is in contradistinction to the first four kingdoms that are totally of human origin. Despite the technology, progress, earthly wisdom, and achievements of these four imperial realms, they still have a temporal nature and hence are destined to pass away. Only God's Kingdom, and those who are part of it, will last forever (II Peter 3:10-13). Biblical Eschatology describes the transition from the "kingdoms of this world" to the "the Kingdom of our Lord and

---

[1] Arnold Fruchtenbaum, *The Footsteps of the Messiah*, Tustin CA: Ariel Ministries, 1990, page 27.

of His Christ" (Revelation 11:15). Though the transfer of power will be cataclysmic--after all, a stone striking a statue is not going to be a peaceful experience—the arrival of this kingdom will fulfill the yearning of all God's righteous people.

Daniel's presentation of Nebuchadnezzar's Statue gives us a tremendous sweep of world history and prophetic destiny, all highlighting the sovereignty of Almighty God. *"The Most High God is sovereign over the kingdoms of men"* (5:21).

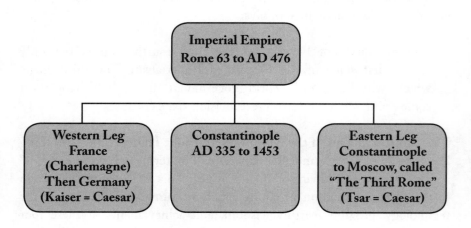

The Five Kingdoms of Daniel			
Chapter Two	Chapter Seven	Chapter Eight	Identity
1. Head of Gold, v. 38	Lion, v. 4		Babylon 626-539 B.C.
2. Chest & Arms of Silver, v. 39	Bear, v. 5	Ram, v. 3-4,20	Medo-Persia 539-331 B.C.
3. Belly & Thigh Bronze, v. 39	Leopard, v. 6	Goat, v. 5-8	Greece or Hellenism of (including Hasomoneans) 331-63B.C.
4. Legs of Iron, Feet of Iron & Clay a. United b. Two-Division c. Ten Division, v. 40	Terrifying & Frightening Beast, v. 7, 23-25 a. United b. One World Government c. Ten Division d. Antichrist	"Little Horn", v. 9-12	Rome 63 B.C. -476 A.D. and beyond
5. Messianic Kingdom: Fills the whole earth and abides forever —2:34, 35, 44, 45			

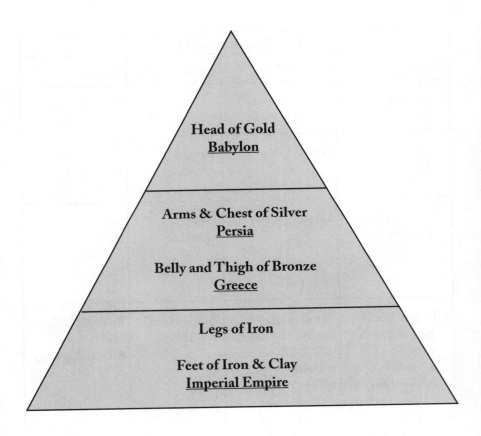

REVIEW QUESTIONS:

1. From memory, name the four types of metal in Nebuchadnezzar's statue and the empires each one represents.
2. In modern times, what has to happen to the East-West balance of power before a one-world government can emerge?

Chapter Six

A Sure Foundation Part III: Book of Daniel
And The Seventy Week Prophecy

The Messiah, the timing of His coming, His crucifixion, antichrist, the abomination of desolation, the Great Tribulation and overflowing judgements. These are spectacular topics, from which spring much end time teaching.

Now imagine this: all these fascinating topics are introduced within a matter of a mere four verses--verses that form the foundation stone of end-time prophetic events. Without them, it would be impossible to properly understand New Testament prophetic passages like the Olivet Discourse or the Book of Revelation.

Just as the Book of Daniel is the foundational book of end-time prophecy, so these four verses from chapter 9: 24, 25, 26, and 27, are the nucleus. We do have a label for these verses. They are called "The Seventy Week Prophecy."

Stan Telchin, author of *Betrayed*, tells the story of how he, a Jewish insurance man, tried to use the Bible to disprove the Messiahship of Jesus to his recently converted daughter. Once he came to Daniel 9, he stumbled. Right before his eyes was the proof that Jesus of Nazareth came to Israel at the right time in history, as the prophet spoke.

Let us take a look at this extraordinary prophecy and see for yourself why God is very much in control of world events.

Background to the Prophecy

God had promised the descendents of Abraham that He would give them in the land of milk and honey—the Promised Land of Canaan--which He did under the leadership of Joshua. But Israel had not been faithful to the Lord, despite much divine blessing and repeated prophetic warnings. So God punished them with the long-promised exile in a strange land, namely Babylon. Psalm 137 says that by the rivers of Babylon, they sat down and wept when they remembered Zion.

In tandem with God's judgement for Israel's sin was His promise of grace, restoration, and mercy. In fact, one of the major prophetic motifs of the Old Testament was condemnation and consolation, judgement and mercy, exile and return. For example, the Prophet Jeremiah predicted Judah's deportation to Babylon and yet he also said that the Jews would return to Judah after seventy years of Babylonian exile. After all, the God of the Bible has a heart for redemption, not rejection.

Daniel 9:24 says the Seventy Weeks is "for your people and for your holy city." Who were Daniel's people? Israel. What was Daniel's holy city? Jerusalem.

Since God fulfilled His promise to deport a rebellious Judah, would He also keep His promise to return them to Jerusalem after seventy years? Would the glory of God ever return to the Temple? These questions represented the longing of every faithful Judean in exile.

Daniel had done his sums and realized that the seventy year captivity in Babylon would soon be over (Jeremiah 25:11-12; 29:10-14). At this point, however, there was no indication that the promised return to the land was even on the calendar. Daniel expected it to be literally fulfilled, but he was not going to passively wait for it to happen. He proactively began to seek the Lord in humility, faith, prayer, fasting, sackcloth, and ashes (9:3) so that the Jews would have the opportunity to return to Jerusalem.

In the midst of his prayer, while confessing his sins and the sins of his people, the Archangel Gabriel appears. He reassures Daniel that he is much beloved, and that as soon as he began to pray, the answer was on the way. But the answer is more than just about a return from exile to Jerusalem; Gabriel is basically giving Daniel the God's prophetic agenda from now, until the coming of the Messiah and the advent of God's Kingdom. This has become known to the world as the "Seventy Week Prophecy."

Daniel 9:24-27 (NKJV)

24 Seventy weeks are determined for your people and for your holy city, to finish the transgression, to make an end of sins, to make reconciliation for iniquity, to bring in everlasting righteousness, to seal up vision and prophecy, and to anoint the Most Holy. 25 Know therefore and understand, that from the going forth of the command to restore and build Jerusalem until Messiah the Prince, there shall be seven weeks and sixty-two weeks; the street shall be built again, and the wall, even in troublesome times. 26 And after the sixty-two weeks Messiah shall be cut off, but not for Himself; and the people of the prince who is to come shall destroy the city and the sanctuary. The end of it shall be with a flood, and till the end

---

[1] In Numbers 14:34 the concept of a year for a day is mentioned, when God condemned the unbelieving generation who left Egypt to spend forty years in the wilderness, because the twelve spies spent forty days in Canaan.

of the war desolations are determined. 27 Then he shall confirm a covenant with many for one week; but in the middle of the week He shall bring an end to sacrifice and offering. And on the wing of abominations shall be one who makes desolate, even until the consummation, which is determined, is poured out on the desolate.

Are They Really "Weeks"

In any serious study, it is vitally important that, before all else, you define the "key terms." Probably no term means more than the word "weeks" because within this timeframe God is going to do some extraordinary things, like make an end of sins. So if we are to understand this prophecy, we need to know the meaning of "weeks."

If God really intended to accomplish the six outcomes of verse 24 in a mere seventy weeks, or sixteen months, then this is an ambitious agenda. The original Hebrew says *shuv'im shiv'im* which literally means "seventy 'seven's'". It is the word "seven's" that is translated "weeks."

In reality, "weeks" is not the correct translation. To say that after the command to restore and rebuild Jerusalem God would fulfil these six conditions in sixteen months <u>and</u> that Messiah, antichrist, abomination of desolations, etc. would appear, is simply not tenable.

So what does "seven's" really mean? If each day of the "week" was turned to a "year," then the seven days in the week would become seven years.[1] The generally accepted interpretation is that "seven's" mean a seven-year period. Seventy "seven year" periods equal 490 years. Remember Jesus used this phrase "seventy times seven" when speaking about how often we must forgive (Matthew 18:22). Because we are dealing with units of seven years, it will be for this reason that the concept of a "seven year tribulation" comes from Daniel, since such a time frame is not mentioned in Revelation.

This interpretation means that Messiah's predicted coming would be around the first century A.D. During that period there was great expectation among the Jewish people that He would appear—which He did! He just did not come in the form they were expecting.

Even though it is inaccurate and potentially misleading to call this prophecy, "Daniel's Seventy Weeks," the term "weeks" has been used so often that it has stuck. Scholars do know what it really means and by now we would probably be lost without it.

For Whom Is This Prophecy?

This question is easy to answer. Verse 24 says it is *"for your people and for your holy city."* Who were Daniel's people? Israel. What was Daniel's holy city? Jerusalem.

Considering this is a passage about the last days, this is truly remarkable. One hundred and fifty years ago Israel did not exist as a geo-political entity and Jerusalem was a small, walled up Turkish village. The only interest and conflict it would stir up was among the fleas and flies. Yet today, both Israel and Jerusalem are at the centre stage of the world's most intractable and dangerous international hot spot, subject of numerous United Nations resolutions, and high up on the agenda of all major western foreign affairs departments.

> *Daniel 9:24 says the Seventy Weeks is "for your people and for your holy city." Who were Daniel's people? Israel. What was Daniel's holy city? Jerusalem.*

It is important that when interpreting this prophecy, we bear in mind to whom it is intended. As such, we will avoid needless error in terms of inspiration and application.

What Will God Do In The Seventy Weeks (9:24)?

Six outcomes will be accomplished by the end of this period of seventy sevens or 490 years. They are as follows:

1. *"To finish the transgression":* this is not just regular sin, but something major. The Hebrew word "pasha" means revolt or rebellion. What was the biggest or most serious revolt or rebellion that Israel did at Jerusalem? Was it not the rejection of Jesus the Messiah (Isaiah 53:1-9; Zechariah 12:10-13:1)? "The transgression" will be finished in the time of the end (Isaiah 59:20 and Romans 11:26).

2. *"To make an end of sins":* this has to do with daily sins, not the big-ticket sins. The idea is that regular sinning will be locked up and contained. When does this happen? After the Messiah returns (Ezek. 36:24-30; 37:24-27; 43:7; Zech. 14). In the future, the Spirit of repentance will be poured out upon Israel and a fountain for sin and uncleanness will be opened to the nation; all Israel shall be saved (Zech. 12:10-13; 11:25-29).

3. *"To make reconciliation for iniquity":* The Hebrew for iniquity is avon, meaning "crooked" or "perverse." Reconciliation is kaphar, where we get "atonement," to cover. Jesus did precisely this at the Cross for Israel and the world (Isaiah 53; Col. 1:20; 2:14-17; I Pet. 2:24). Israel, collectively, has not yet experienced this due to "the transgression," but it will be accomplished at the Second Coming of Christ (Isaiah 1:18-20; 66:7-8; Zechariah 12:10-13:1; Matthew 23:37-39; Romans 11:25-29).

4. *"To bring in everlasting righteousness":* When the first three outcomes are fulfilled, then an age of righteousness will begin, known also as the Messianic Kingdom (Isaiah 9:6-7; 12:1-6; Daniel 2:44-45; 7:13-14,18,27; Ezekiel 43:7; Zechariah 14; Luke 1:32-33; Romans 11:25-29; Revelation 11:15; 19:11-20:10).

5. *"To seal up the vision and prophecy":* Prophecies concerning Israel and Jerusalem will be fulfilled completely when the Messiah returns. Vision may refer to oral prophecies like Elijah and Elisha while prophecies pertain to those things written like the five major and twelve minor prophets of the Old Testament.

6. *"To anoint the most holy":* Not one hundred percent sure, but most likely this refers to a place rather than a person. The concept is the cleansing of the holy of holies, the Temple, and Jerusalem from the horrendous sacrilege of the abomination of desolation and then anointing the "fourth" or "millennial" temple of the Messianic kingdom (Zech. 40-43; Zechariah 6:12-13).

When Do The Seventy Weeks Start (9:25)?

This verse starts off with an imperative command: <u>know and understand!</u> If you do not get the timing right, you could miss the train. Amazingly, we actually have a time frame of when Jesus Christ will appear: at the end of two time periods, "seven seven's" and "sixty-two sevens" or sixty nine weeks (483 years). How tragic it would be to miss the coming of the Messiah just because one did not know how to tell the time, even though they wore an accurate watch!

The starting point is the command to *"restore and rebuild Jerusalem."* When and by whom did this command happen? There were three decrees, all given by Persian monarchs, regarding Jerusalem:

1. **Cyrus the Great:** In the first year of his reign the command to restore and rebuild the Temple was given (Ezra 1:1-4; 3:8; Isaiah 44:28; 45:1-4; 46:11). He reigned from 538 B.C. for nine years and his son Cambyses reigned for seven years. Due to local opposition, the work of the Temple ceased (Ezra 4:1-24).

2. **Darius I:** In the second year of his thirty-five year reign he confirmed the decree of Cyrus, made eighteen years earlier. The Temple was finished in the sixth year of his reign, but Jerusalem was not restored, even during the twenty-one year reign of Xerxes (Daniel 11:1-3).

3. **Artaxerxes:** In the twentieth year of his reign the king gave Nehemiah authorization to rebuild "the city of my father's tombs," namely Jerusalem. The year is around 457 B.C. and it is from this date that the countdown of the "Seventy Weeks" begins. The "street"

and the "wall" will be rebuilt in troublesome times. This is precisely what Nehemiah did. He rebuilt the walls in a record fifty-two days, though this may not have been the complete restoration that was envisaged.

While some commentators prefer to start the Seventy Week countdown with Cyrus' decree, the problem is that:

a) Cyrus gave a command to rebuild the Temple, not *"restore and build Jerusalem"*

b) It would set the dating out by as much as eighty years.

The "seven sevens" and "sixty-two" after this verse means 483 years, and when you add them together, we end up at A.D. 26, which is around the time of Jesus' ministry.

What Is the Three-Fold Division of the Seventy Weeks (9:25)?

A. **"Seven sevens" or forty-nine years:** This would take us to around 408 B.C. Was there anything significant about this year? It is not easy to tell, however, there are two options. First, after forty-nine years the city of Jerusalem was completely restored: streets, walls, everything. Second, this year could represent the end of Malachi's ministry, and thus the completion of the canon of the Old Testament.

B. **"Sixty-two sevens or four hundred and thirty four years:** This period goes from 408 B.C. until A.D. 26. This clearly represents the intertestamental period--the era between the Old and New Testaments--which are full of important activities. Old Testament era ends with Persia (chest and arms of silver) as the international masters but when the curtain rises in the New Testament, Rome (legs of iron) is in charge. Between these two is the Hellenistic empire, with the flourishing of Greek language, philosophy, and culture throughout the whole of the Old Persian Empire. Hellenism was so potent and attractive that Rome adopted much of it into its body politic, thus fostering Greco-Roman culture. Since Jesus was born at least two years before the death of Herod the Great in 4 B.C., He could very well have been age thirty-three by the year A.D. 26.

C. **"One seven" or seven years:** More will be said about this in a moment but this represents the period of the Great Tribulation.

TIMELINE

| 7 Weeks (49 years) | 62 Weeks (434 years) | Church Age | 70th Week |

457 B.C. - 408 B.C. I 408 B.C. to A.D. 26 I AD 26 to Present I Tribulation

Messiah, the Crucifixion, and the Aftermath (9:26)

After the "seven seven's" and the "sixty-two seven's," which makes a total of sixty-nine sevens or 483 years, two things will happen:

1. **Messiah:** The term "Messiah" is introduced for the first, and only, time in the English Bible, both 9:25 and 26. He is called "Messiah the Prince," which is fitting as the heir of the house of David. This Son of David will fulfil the tenets of the Davidic covenant and rule from his throne perpetually.

   However, Daniel introduces a new and terrifying twist: Messiah the Prince will actually be cut off! How can someone, who will rule and reign forever, be killed, and especially in such a violent manner?

   This has understandably become a stumbling block, until one understands the whole of Scripture. In the Hebrew the word *karath* means to "cut off to death," which is also the term used to make a covenant "*karath ha brit*" or "cut a covenant." If this word *karath* also implies crucifixion, it makes the death of the Messiah all the more outlandish, because Deuteronomy 21:23 says cursed is everyone who hangs on a tree (also quoted in Galatians 3:13). Messiah will be "*cut off, but not for Himself*" (Isaiah 53:8; I Peter 2:21), which sounds exactly like the mission of Jesus, to die for the sins of the world.

2. **Jerusalem Destroyed:** Remember that earlier in this chapter, Daniel had been interceding for the return of his people from exile and the restoration of Jerusalem. Now, Gabriel is telling him that Jerusalem will be destroyed.

At the time of this prophecy, Jerusalem was already in ruins due to Nebuchadnezzar's conquest back in 586 B.C. But what happens in this prophecy, Jerusalem will be rebuilt by another generation and destroyed by another people. The key phrase here is *"the people of the prince who is to come"* (Matt. 22:7) are the ones who will destroy "the city and the sanctuary" (Luke 19:43-44).

Which destruction and which people is the text talking about? Fortunately, there is very little disagreement on this point. Historically, the next wholesale demolition of Jerusalem and the Temple was by the Romans in A.D. 70. So the "Roman people" destroyed the city and sanctuary and it is from their ranks that a "prince" will come, the one apparently alluded to in verse 27. While it is popular to say that this prince will be Roman (and many a pope in history has been nominated as such), if we take Fruchtenbaum's term of "imperial empire," which spanned Southern Europe, North Africa, and the Middle East, that gives more space for an evil end-time prince to emerge.

The final phrase of this verse, *"The end of it shall be with a flood, and till the end of the war desolations are determined"* may have applied to the First Jewish Revolt against Rome from A.D. 66-70 (Masada fell three years later). The term "flood" could be figurative for a military invasion, which is what Titus did to Jerusalem in A.D. 70. Or, it may harmonize more with

> *How tragic it would be to miss the coming of the Messiah just because one did not know how to tell the time, even though they wore an accurate watch!*

the end of this age and the tribulation, since "*wars and rumours of wars*" are earth's plight until the end of the age.

The Gap?

Conservative commentators have insisted that there is a gap, even a lengthy one, between the end of the sixty-ninth week and the beginning of the seventieth. The other theory is called *continuous view*, which says that there are no gaps and Daniel's seventieth week was fulfilled during the first seven years of church history.

Some have questioned on what basis can we insert a gap? It is a fair question, and in answering it causes us to look at the broad sweep of Scripture.

First, the concept of a gap or breach is nothing new. Liken it to pressing a pause button on a player, which holds the action, until the pause button is pressed again. While Scripture can write about prophetic events as if they all happen at once, there have been "gap" precedents. A gap exists between:

- The Patriarchs entering the land and their descendents inheriting it under Joshua;

- Jacob promising his son Judah a sceptre and the first Judean king David inheriting the throne;

- The first and second comings of the Messiah;

- The Day of the Lord;

- The two resurrections, of the righteous and unrighteous;

- Israel's blindness and Israel's salvation

Second, to accept the continuous view theory is to say that the six conditions of verse 24 have been fulfilled, that the "abomination of desolations" occurred, that sacrifices and offerings ceased, that the consummation of the end is fulfilled, that the covenant was broken halfway, etc.

What is the scorecard seven years after Christ's death and resurrection, the continuous view's seventieth week? The end of sins and transgressions has not yet come (there would be plenty more in the future). The Jewish sacrificial system in the Jerusalem Temple continued unabated for over forty years after the resurrection of Jesus. The veil of the Temple, supernaturally torn during Christ's crucifixion was, in all probability, replaced. In A.D. 70 there was no abomination of desolation when the Temple was destroyed, yet Christ makes it clear that one will come (Matthew 24:15). Have we seen a broken covenant three and a half years after the resurrection? Has the end of the age come? Did Christ institute a covenant at the cross, only to break it after three and a half years?

The answers should be obvious.

The simple, straightforward, and literal explanation is that there is a gap between God's dealings with Israel and Jerusalem in the first sixty-nine weeks and that of the seventieth week. So what is in between these two periods? The Church Age. This is why literal interpreters argue that Daniel 9:24-27 has nothing to do with the church, but with Israel.

If this is the case, then basically when the Church was born on the Day of Pentecost (Acts 2), the 70 Week time clock paused. The whole flow of Church history ensued. Then when the Church is removed at the Rapture (I Thessalonians 4), the Seventy Week time clock can be reactivated to allow the Seventieth (70th) Week to be fulfilled.

At the same time, God's dealings with Israel had changed because of their unbelief. They were broken off and the city of Jerusalem destroyed, as was prophesied by both Daniel and Jesus (Daniel 9:26; Matthew 21:43; 23:37-39; 24:2; Luke 21:20-24, Acts 13:45-49; Romans 11). So the primacy of Israel in the dealings of God had been temporarily paused and a new people of God, made of redeemed Jews and Gentiles, took their place. But the natural branches, broken off due to unbelief, will be grafted back into the tree. When that happens, it shall be life from the dead (Romans 11:15).

Some strenuously object to the notion that the church is some parenthetical insertion in what is God's plan for Israel. Let it be stressed that the church is neither a parenthesis nor afterthought in the mind of God; it was ordained from before the foundation of the world. Its emergence was hinted at in Genesis 12:3 where it says all the nations of the earth shall be blessed through Abraham.

The church constitutes redeemed Jews and redeemed Gentiles since the Day of Pentecost until the Second Coming. No more division exists between the Jew and the Gentile "in Christ." We believe the mystery of the church was concealed in the Old Testament and revealed in the New. It was first anticipated after Peter confessed Jesus as the Messiah. The

Lord responded by saying that He would "build His Church" (Matthew 16:18). So there is no demotion of the glorious place the Church enjoys in the economy of God.

Let us remember to whom this prophecy is written? Israel and Jerusalem.

The Seventieth Week (9:27)

Traditionally this is considered to be the seven year tribulation period, which is amplified in the Book of Revelation (which, as was mentioned earlier, never uses the phrase seven years). The "prince" of the people, namely antichrist, will make a covenant with "many" for one week. It is the signing of the covenant, not the rapture, that kick-starts the seventieth week. Israel will be back in the land. Those Israelis, who have returned from the Diaspora, will enter into this agreement. Apparently, there will be offerings and sacrifices made. These can only be done at the Jewish Temple, which can only be built at the Temple Mount in Jerusalem. Will antichrist allow the rebuilding of the Jerusalem Temple and the reinstitution of animal sacrifices? If you take the prophecy literally, the answer appears to be "yes."

At the moment, all this appears impossible. The temple site is now Muslim property called the *Haram esh Sharif* (translated the "Noble Sanctuary") and houses the Dome of the Rock and Al Aqsa Mosque. These are the prizes of the Muslim world and protected by Israeli law. The prospects of serious violence and warfare are very high if they were touched or removed. In addition, the Jewish people are no longer in the habit of temple sacrifices, and many in Israel are not even observant. If this passage is to be literally fulfilled, then antichrist has to be persuasively powerful to push through the rebuilding of the temple, a diabolical counterfeit to Cyrus the Great.

In the middle of the seventieth week, he breaks the covenant, causes the sacrifices to cease, and sets up the abomination of desolation (Matthew 24:15; II Thessalonians 2:4). This period lasts three and a half years. While Antiochus IV fulfilled this in 168-165 B.C., Jesus Christ two hundred years later affirmed it as a future event. Antichrist will deny opportunity to worship the true God, demand worship of himself, and seek to destroy all those who refuse to cooperate. This will continue "...*until the consummation, which is determined is poured out on the desolate*" or, as the NIV says, "...*until the end that is decreed is poured out on him*" (Daniel 9:27). This "prince to come," antichrist does have a foreordained end and it will come fully and forcefully.

With Daniel's Seventy Week prophecy as a framework, let us see how it helps us to understand Bible prophecy from a New Testament point-of-view.

REVIEW QUESTIONS:

1. How many conditions need to be fulfilled by the end of the seventy weeks?
2. Where, and for whom, is this prophecy directed?
3. Regarding the 70th week, explain the difference between the gap theory versus continuous view theory.

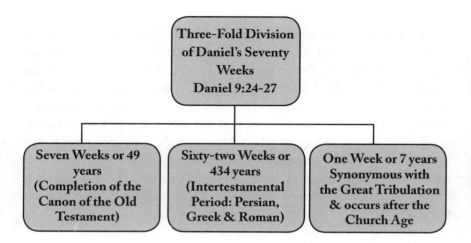

Part Three

Theological Theories

Chapter Seven

Rapture Theories

1 Thessalonians 4:13-18 (NKJV)

13 But I do not want you to be ignorant, brethren, concerning those who have fallen asleep, lest you sorrow as others who have no hope.14 For if we believe that Jesus died and rose again, even so God will bring with Him those who sleep in Jesus.15 For this we say to you by the word of the Lord, that we who are alive and remain until the coming of the Lord will by no means precede those who are asleep.16 For the Lord Himself will descend from heaven with a shout, with the voice of an archangel, and with the trumpet of God. And the dead in Christ will rise first.17 Then we who are alive and remain shall be caught up together with them in the clouds to meet the Lord in the air. And thus we shall always be with the Lord.18 Therefore comfort one another with these words.

The above passage describes the event that every Christian should long for with great intensity: the coming of Christ for His church. As mentioned earlier in this book, everyone agrees that Christ is coming again and that when He returns, we will be with Him forever. These verses make it impossible to believe otherwise. Nevertheless, the event described is popularly called "the rapture" and, far from being a unifying doctrine, it has caused heated debate. This is not unusual, when you consider other important issues like Holy Communion, water baptism, eternal security, and speaking in tongues, also generate a lot of controversy.

In this chapter, we are going to look at this doctrine more closely and look at the various rapture theories. Remember that "valid uncertainties" help explain why there are disagreements in the timing of the rapture, but these should never be outside of Christian love and care. If so, there is something seriously wrong with one's brand of Christianity.

Rapture Defined

I Thessalonians 4:17 uses the phrase "shall be caught up together" and this is where we get the notion of rapture. The original Greek for "caught up" is *harpazo*, in full, *harpagesometha* which is the passive mood, future tense of *harpazo*. The actual word "rapture" comes from the Latin Vulgate (A.D. 405), which uses the Latin verb rapere. It means, "take forcefully, abduct, seize, carry off, pluck, pull, and take by force."

Since the passage does not tell the timing of the rapture, there have been various interpretations. After all, is there a distinction between the Rapture and the Second Coming of Christ? Are they the same event or are they separated by a period of time?

The Case Against and For the Rapture

While there is no argument that Christ will return, considerable debate remains as to whether there will be a return "for" the saints (rapture) preceding a return "with" the saints (second coming). Will Christ come for the church before the end of the world?

Opponents claim that the rapture is a "new" theory from the nineteenth century and is not part of apostolic teaching. If it were such an important doctrine, surely Christ would have highlighted it clearly. Furthermore, there appears to be no Scriptures that imply that the church will be absent from earth following a rapture.

Roman Catholics and many Protestants reject the notion of a separate rapture from the Second Coming. They believe that I Thessalonians 4:16-17 will happen at the time of the general resurrection and Judgement Day, when the saints will rise to meet Christ as He comes to earth as its Judge. The Eastern Orthodox Church, who also rejects the rapture, says that according to passages like Isaiah, the earth will be renewed and the Kingdom of Heaven will physically reside here. So no one will be going up.

Supporters of the rapture use two passages:

Matthew 24:40-41

40 "Then two men will be in the field: one will be taken and the other left. 41 "Two women will be grinding at the mill: one will be taken and the other left.

Philippians 3:21

21 who will transform our lowly body that it may be conformed to His glorious body, according to the working by which He is able even to subdue all things to Himself.

They argue that just because a doctrine is newly-revealed does not make it unacceptable. Revelation of God's truth can be progressive. For example, the Old Testament barely mentions the doctrine of resurrection or of a New Testament-style church, but yet they are accepted, even celebrated doctrines today. When it comes to prophetic passages, it is even possible that key passages will not make sense until the time of the end. Daniel 12:4

(NKJV) says, *"But you, Daniel, shut up the words, and seal the book until the time of the end...."* Christ's phrase "just like the days of Noah" implies that while life goes on and intensifies, something dramatic will happen that will separate people in a permanent way, as Matthew 24:40-41 imply.

People's eschatology is often determined by the times and culture in which they live. Those living in fourth century Constantinople could be forgiven for thinking they were already in the Millennium, if not heaven, because of the grandeur of the imperial city. The choir in the renowned Hagia Sophia, or the Cathedral of Holy Wisdom, sounded like the angelic hosts. Therefore, they would have balked at the notion of a future, Jewish-flavoured millennium (as is premillennialism), when the millennium was so clearly happening now.

As we look at the various rapture theories, remember that your eschatology will be determined by the previously mentioned three "I" questions:

1. **Interpretation:** How literally to you interpret Scripture, both the individual passage and the total context?

2. **Imminence:** How imminent is Christ's return? Can He come at any time or do certain signs need to be fulfilled first?

3. **Israel:** Do Israel and the Jewish people have a part, even a major part, in end-time prophetic events?

Post-Tribulation Rapture Theory

The Church of Christ will remain on earth until the Second Coming of Christ and the end of the age: the rapture and Christ's Second Coming take place at the same time. This means that the Church of the last generation will go through the Great Tribulation described in Revelation.

Their arguments in favour of this position include:

1. **New Theory:** Pre-Tribulation Rapture theory is a relatively new doctrine from John Nelson Darby and the Plymouth Brethren in the 1830's.

2. **Position of the Early Church:** Post-tribulationism and a church in the tribulation was the position of the early church. Matthew 24:22 mentions "saints" in the tribulation, so they must be present during this terrible period.

3. **Tribulation Promised:** The church has always been promised tribulation (John 16:33). This does not preclude the fact that the church can be protected during this period.

4. **No Imminence:** They say that signs must be fulfilled first before Christ can return. Matthew 24:14 say that the Gospel must be preached in the whole world as a witness before the end can come.

5. **Daniel's Seventy Weeks:** This is considered to have been fulfilled in history, thus adopting 'continuous view.'

6. **Same Words:** Words for the rapture and Second Coming are the same (compare Matthew 24:27 to I Thessalonians 4:15). Rapture and Resurrection: The biggest argument is the resurrection of the holy dead at the rapture (I Thessalonians 4:16) or where there is a resurrection, there is also a rapture.

Opponents of this theory point out that "newness" of doctrine in no way makes it illegitimate provided it is consistent with the tenor of all of Scripture. As such, post-tribulationists are accused of mixing the church, which has no part of Daniel's Seventy Weeks, with the Jews. The tribulation is the seventieth week. Similar words are easy to explain because the two events are similar, but held at different times. While the church has been told there is tribulation, it has also been promised to be protected from God's wrath (I Thessalonians 5:9), which is a major component of the Great Tribulation.

Arguments against Christ's imminent return are attacked because the church is told to look for the coming of Jesus, not for end-time signs. Regarding the resurrection argument, opponents say that there is one resurrection but in several stages, citing I Corinthians 15:23 "...every man in his own order." This means that within the first resurrection is the resurrection of Jesus Christ, followed by the church saints, Old Testament saints, and then tribulation saints. All of these are raised at a different time, "in his own order," but are still part of the blessed first resurrection. Matthew 24 is considered to be written to the Jews, as was the whole Gospel, and hence references to things like "Sabbath travel" and those living in "Judea." These people are told to flee. But in Luke's gospel, written to the Gentiles by a Gentile, they are not told to flee but "...*look up and lift up your heads, because your redemption draws near*" (21:28).

Mid-Tribulation Rapture

The church will face the afflictions of the first half of Daniel's seventieth week, but raptured before the greater tribulation, which is the outpouring of God's wrath. Like post-tribulationists, they do not believe in the imminent return of Christ. Like pre-tribulationists, they see the rapture and the second coming as two separate events.

Arguments For:

1. **"Last Trump" equals "Seventh Trumpet:** This is their key argument. I Corinthians 15:52 says that the rapture will occur at the "last trumpet." Mid-tribulationists say this is the same as the seventh trumpet of Revelation 11:15.

2. **The Two Witnesses:** The resurrection of the two witnesses in Revelation 11:11 is in the middle of the tribulation. It represents the rapture of the entire church.

3. **Deliverance from Wrath:** The church is not promised deliverance from tribulation, which is the affliction of antichrist, but from the wrath of God (Rev. 11:2; 12:6), which is a result of the tribulation.

Arguments Against:

The seventh trumpet from Revelation 8 and 9, as well as all other trumpets, has nothing to do with the rapture of the church but with judgement of unbelievers. In fact, the seventh trumpet is actually known as the Third Woe Judgement (Revelation 11:14). Within the seventh trumpet are the entire seven bowl judgements, which stretch out to the end of Daniel's 70th Week. With such announcements as *"the kingdoms of this world have become the kingdoms of our Lord and of His Christ, and He shall reign forever and ever"* (Revelation 11:15), it can be argued that the second trumpet begins at the mid-tribulation period but goes to the end of the great tribulation, where a change of kingdoms occur.

Partial Rapture Theory

Partial rapture means that only those believers who are "worthy" will be taken from the world by the Lord, while carnal, two-timing, sin-loving Christians will remain behind to be purified through the great tribulation. Some partial rapturists teach that regularly there will be raptures throughout the tribulation; once a believer has been made clean, they are able to go up in to heaven to be with the Lord.

Argument For:

"So Christ was offered once to bear the sins of many. To those who eagerly wait for Him He will appear a second time, apart from sin, for salvation" (Hebrews 9:28)

Utilizing the above verse, this appears to imply one needs to be prepared in order meet the Lord. It helps to fulfill God's promise to preserve the church from tribulation, while fulfilling Ephesians injunction that Christ is coming for a glorious church, without spot or wrinkle (Ephesians 5:27). It creates an incentive for holy living.

Argument Against:

Apart from the fact that there is little scriptural support, this theory seems to imply that there are two types of Christians and that good works is the key to being raptured. When good works comes into the picture, they are never enough to bring righteousness. Remember that the Corinthians were a carnal group of Christians, yet Paul tells them *"we shall all be changed"* (I Corinthians 15:51). The Shepherd is returning for all of His flock, the white sheep and the black sheep.

Pre-Tribulation Rapture

The Church of Christ will not go through the Great Tribulation, which is the same as Daniel's Seventieth Week. Israel and Jerusalem are subjects of this week, whereas the church will be saved from the wrath to come.

Arguments For:

1. **Imminence:** One of the key practical issues of Eschatology is what exactly is a believer to do? And for what should he or she await? The doctrine of imminence says that the believer should not be looking for antichrist, the whore of Babylon, marks of the beast, or other end time signs, but for the coming of the Lord. Scriptures for imminence include:

   - Titus 2:13 *"looking for the blessed hope and glorious appearing of our great God and Savior Jesus Christ"*
   - Luke 12:35 *"Let your waist be girded and your lamps burning;"*

- <u>Matthew 24:42</u> *"Watch therefore, for you do not know what hour your Lord is coming."*
- <u>Matthew 24:44</u> *"Therefore you also be ready, for the Son of Man is coming at an hour you do not expect."*
- <u>1 Peter 1:13</u> *"Therefore gird up the loins of your mind, be sober, and rest your hope fully upon the grace that is to be brought to you at the revelation of Jesus Christ;"*
- Other passages that allude to imminence-the Christ could return at any moment without warning--include Acts 1:11; 1 Corinthians 1:7; 15:51-52; 16:22; Philippians 3:20; 4:5; Colossians 3:4; I Thessalonians 1:10, Titus 2:13; I Timothy 6:4; Hebrews 9:28; James 5:7-9; I Peter 3:3-4; Jude 21; Revelation 3:11; 22:7, 12, 17, 20.

Without question life on this planet will become darker and darker for those who do not believe. But, paradoxically, it will actually become lighter and brighter for the followers of Christ (Isaiah 60:1-2; Proverbs 4:18-19). While the preaching of the Word and the collective light of the saints will shine brightly, what could bring the brightest light of all than the actual return of Jesus Christ, the light of the world (John 8:12)? Only a pre-tribulation rapture can uphold the doctrine of Christ's imminent and unexpectedness of the return of Christ for His saints, since all other theories demand signs to be fulfilled first.

Regarding imminence, Dr. Renal Showers says:
The fact that the glorified, holy Son of God could step through the door of heaven at any moment is intended by God to be the most

pressing, incessant motivation for holy living and aggressive ministry (including missions, evangelism and Bible teaching) and the greatest cure for lethargy and apathy. It should make a major difference in every Christian's values, actions, priorities and goals.[1]

2. **Preservation from the Coming Wrath:** While believers can expect tribulation in this world (John 16:33), they have every reason to believe that God will preserve them from the time of wrath. Since the nature of the tribulation is a time of wrath (Rev. 6:17)--both the God's and the devil's--believers can look to God for protection, as He has promised in His word. Promises of protection include:

Romans 5:9; 1 Thessalonians 1:10; 5:9

- <u>Romans 5:9</u> *Much more then, having now been justified by His blood, we shall be saved from wrath through Him.10 and to wait for His Son from heaven, whom He raised from the dead, even Jesus who delivers us from the wrath to come.*

- <u>I Thessalonians 5:9</u> *For God did not appoint us to wrath, but to obtain salvation through our Lord Jesus Christ*

Yes, it is possible for God to protect His people throughout the time of wrath, like the Ark protected Noah and his family during the flood. But as you read Revelation 3:10, is God protecting us "through" wrath or "from" wrath?

---

[1] Renal Showers, *Maranatha*, page 256, as found in Thomas Ice and Timothy Demy, *Fast Facts on Bible Prophecy,* Eugene OR: Harvest House Publishers, 1997, page 160.

...I also will keep you from the hour of trial which shall come upon the whole world, to test those who dwell on the earth."

The question is whether God is merely protecting Philadelphia during the tribulation period, or removing them altogether from the earth, which will be completely touched by wrath?

Some Pre-Tribulation Rapturists argue that, like John, the church is going up because there is no mention of the church after Revelation 4:1, when God commands John to come up and view the future events.

3. **Literal Interpretation:** Without question the pre-tribulation rapture theory, along with premillennialism, is the most literal of all theories, even with the symbolic language of Daniel and Revelation notwithstanding. Some of the reasons for this include:

   A. **The Theocratic Covenants:** Abrahamic, Palestinian, Davidic, and New Covenants are taken literally, unconditionally, and prophetically. They apply to Israel and those portions not fulfilled in the Biblical age or church age will find their fulfilment in the Kingdom Age, known also as the millennium. Indeed, a millennium would be necessary just to house the unfulfilled provisions of these covenants, like the land boundaries of Israel from the river of Egypt to the river Euphrates (Gen 15:18), something that has not yet happened.

   B. **Israel and the Church:** Literal interpretation and the Pre-Tribulation Rapture Theory demand that there be a distinction between the two peoples of God, one natural, earthly, and yet to be saved; the other spiritual, heavenly, and fully saved. Theocratic covenant provisions and the Seventy Week prophecy apply to Israel. The church does not have a part of any of Daniel's 70 Weeks, and that includes the last and final 70th week, which is about the Tribulation. From Israel's Old Testament point-of-view, the church is a mystery (Ephesians 3:10-17; Romans 16:25-27; Colossians 1:26-29); and as such, has no part in any of Daniel's Seventy Weeks.

Also the tribulation is referred to as the "time of "Jacob's Trouble" (Jeremiah 30:7), not the church's trouble. So while the church does not want to encroach on the literal aspects of Israel's covenantal blessings, neither does it want or need to inherit any part of Jacob's trouble, a time a of wrath, indignation, and punishment; things God promised to preserve the true church from.

ISRAEL & THE CHURCH CONTRASTED[2]		
TOPIC	**ISRAEL**	**THE CHURCH**
Biblical Revelation	Four-fifths	One-fifth
Divine purpose	Earthly promises /covenants	Heavenly promises in the Gospel
Seed of Abraham	Physical to spiritual	Spiritual seed
Headship	Abraham	Christ
Covenants	All	Indirectly all
Nationality	One nation	All nations
Divine dealings	National, individual	Individual only
Dispensations	Seen in all ages	Only present age
Ministry	No outreach	Great commission
Death of Christ	Guilty nationally	Not guilty at all

---

[2] Dwight Pentecost, *Things to Come*, Grand Rapids, Zondervan, 1964, page 202.

ISRAEL & THE CHURCH CONTRASTED[2]		
TOPIC	**ISRAEL**	**THE CHURCH**
The Father	National relations	Related individual
Christ	Messiah, Immanuel, King	Saviour, Lord, Bridegroom, Head
The Holy Spirit	Came on a few	Comes on all
Governing principle	Mosaic Law	Grace system
Divine enablement	None	Indwelling Spirit
Farewell discourse	Olivet	Upper Room
Return of Christ	Power/glory/Judgement	Receive to Himself
Position	A Servant	Family Member
Christ's Earthly Reign	Subjects	Co-Reigners
Priesthood	Has a priesthood	Is a priesthood
Marriage	Unfaithful wife	Bride
Judgements	Must face	Delivered from In
Eternity	Spirits perfected	Firstborn

4. **Rapture and Second Coming:** This theory makes the clearest distinction between these two events; where in the Rapture Christ is coming **for** the saints and in the Second Coming Christ is coming **with** the saints.

Distinction Between the Rapture and the Second Coming	
Rapture	**Second Coming**
Christ Comes for His Church	Christ Comes With His Church
Can happen at any time (imminent)	Prophetic signs must happen first
Christ appears for the believers	Christ appears to the world
Coming to Comfort	Coming to Judge
Tribulation Follows	Kingdom Follows
Christ Comes in the Air	Christ Comes on Earth
Affects Believers Alone	Affects All People
Believers Taken to Heaven	Believers Taken to the Kingdom
Mystery	Predicted in both Testaments
The Lord at Hand	The Kingdom at Hand

5. **Other Reasons:** These are not primary reasons for the pretribulation case, but they are offered for the sake of interest. Included are:

A. **Interval:** Two key events that will happen when believers meet the Lord include the Judgement Seat of Christ and the Marriage of the Lamb. The former is not a judgement in the sense of punishment, but of receiving rewards for the deeds done in the earthly body. The latter is to fulfil one of the choice reasons for our redemption. An assumption is made that there must be an "interval" of time between the Rapture and Second Coming so that these events can take place. Thus while the earth is experiencing the final affliction of tribulation and antichrist, the saints are receiving their justly earned rewards.

B. **Government:** Scripture makes it clear that believers are not rebels; they obey the temporal authorities (1 Timothy 2:1-4; Romans 13:1-7; Titus 3:1; 1 Peter 2:13-16). How can this be possible when the government during the time of the tribulation will be nothing less than the agent of Satan himself?

C. **Typology:** It is not recommended to make a major doctrine out of typology, even though it does serve an important purpose. But Old Testament typology does provide some ammunition for pre-tribulation rapturists. For example, the preservation of Noah and his family on the Ark, or Lot who was removed from Sodom before the fire and brimstone fell, or Rahab the harlot being spared by the invading Israelites by simply hanging a scarlet cord on the window, are examples used. All of them were preserved through the time of judgement, though only one of them was removed from the arena of judgement before it came. The argument is that if God would go to this extent to preserve mere individuals, how much more will He protect the church which He has purchased with the Blood of Christ!

Since Paul's epistles do not breathe a word about a tribulation-plagued church, then it seems that Luke 21:36 becomes all the more real for the righteous who wait for His coming.

As you consider the wonderful doctrine of Christ's return for His church, remember the most important point is this: Jesus is coming again!

REVIEW QUESTIONS:

1. What does the word "rapture" mean?
2. Is there a difference between the rapture and the Second Coming, and, if so, why?
3. Name the four rapture theories. Which one do you lean towards?

Chapter Eight

Millennium Theories

A time of universal peace and prosperity, where the lion will lie down with the lamb, nations will beat swords and spears into ploughshares and pruning hooks, where the government will be virtuous and the King lives forever. Sounds too good to be true? Welcome to the doctrine of the Millennium.

Despite the pleasant descriptions, this doctrine has been on a theological fault line for centuries. Not all Christians accept that there will be a literal millennium after Christ returns. The debate has been robust, even acrimonious. So what really is the truth about the Millennium?

In this chapter, we will look at the key verses that describe this event, and then explore the major theories involving the Millennium. Let us begin with the key scriptures:

Revelation 19 (NKJV)—Describes the Second Coming

19 And I saw the beast, the kings of the earth, and their armies, gathered together to make war against Him who sat on the horse and against His army. 20 Then the beast was captured, and with him the false prophet who worked signs in his presence, by which he deceived those who received the mark of the beast and those who worshiped his image. These two were cast alive into the lake of fire burning with brimstone. 21 And the rest were killed with the sword, which proceeded from the mouth of Him who sat on the horse. And all the birds were filled with their flesh.

Revelation 20 (NKJV)—Describes the Millennium

*Then I saw an angel coming down from heaven, having the key to the bottomless pit and a great chain in his hand.2 He laid hold of the dragon, that serpent of old, who is the Devil and Satan, and bound him for **a thousand years**; 3 and he cast him into the bottomless pit, and shut him up, and set a seal on him, so that he should deceive the nations no more till **the thousand years** were finished. But after these things he must be released for a little while. 4 And I saw thrones, and they sat on them, and judgement was committed to them. Then I saw the souls of those who had been beheaded for their witness to Jesus and for the word of God, who had not worshiped the beast or his image, and had not received his mark on their foreheads or on their hands. And they lived and reigned with Christ for **a thousand years.** 5 But the rest of the dead did not live again until the thousand years were finished. This is the first resurrection.6 Blessed and holy is he who has part in the first resurrection. Over such **the second death** has no power, but they shall be priests of God and of Christ, and shall reign with Him **a thousand years**. 7 Now when **the thousand years** have expired, Satan will be released from his prison.*

From the above passage you can see that the phrase "**A** thousand years" is used three times (v. 2, 4, and 6) and "**The** thousand years" is also used three times (v. 3, 5, and 7), thus it is used six times in six verses. The key characters include the following:

- An angel (v. 1,2,3)
- Devil (v. 2, 3, 7); also called Dragon v. 2; Satan v. 2,7, and old serpent v. 2
- First Resurrection Saints (v. 4, 6)
- Unrighteous Dead (v. 4)
- The beast (v. 4)
- Christ (v. 4, 6)

The key events of this passage are:

I. Satan Bound (v. 2-3). He is
   A. Grabbed by the angel (v. 2);
   B. Cast into a pit (v. 3);
   C. Shut up in pit (v. 3);
   D. Seal is put on the pit[1] (v. 3);
   E. Cannot deceive during the 1000 years (v. 3);
   F. Loosed for a season (v. 3,7).

II. Martyrs Rise and Reign:
   A. Sit on thrones (v. 4);
   B. Judgement given to them (v. 4);
   C. Beheaded for the witness of Jesus (v. 4);
   D. Beheaded for the word of God (v. 4);
   E. Did not worship the beast (v. 4);
   F. Did not worship his image (v. 4);
   G. Did not receive his mark on their foreheads (v. 4);
   H. Did not receive his mark on their hands (v. 4);
   I. They lived and reigned with Christ a 1,000 years (v. 4);

---

[1] Word used for his location (in Greek abussos = bottomless) refers to the immeasurable underworld, the lowest region of the abode of the dead, the home of demons (cf. Deut 30:13; Rom 10:7; Luke 8:31); it is used seven times in Revelation (9:1,2,11; 11:7; 17:8; 20:1,3). Another name for this place of imprisonment is *Tartarus* (this familiar term from the pagan world is used in II Peter 2:4). Wherever it is, it does not appear to be on earth.

III. First Resurrection (Saints)
   A. Blessed (v. 6);
   B. Holy (v. 6);
   C. Second death has no power (v. 6);
   D. Priests of God and Christ (v. 6);
   E. Shall reign 1000 years (v. 6).

Millennium Summarized in Revelation 20:1-7

1. Satan bound, shut up, sealed, so he cannot deceive the nations while the 1,000 years are in progress.
2. Those who sat on the thrones and John says "and I saw" which implies a group of martyred saints lived and reigned with Christ 1,000 years. Mentioned in verses 4 and 6.
3. Satan loosed after the 1,000 years, verses 3 and 7.
4. First resurrection sees the 1,000 years.
5. Second resurrection does not see the 1,000 years.

The above passages describe the Second Coming and the Millennium. In fact, this is not only the clearest passage about the Millennium, and for some scholars, it is the only passage about the Millennium. If it wasn't for Revelation 20, they lament, there would be no theological debate about the Millennium and our complex lives would be simplified.

We need to remember that Revelation 20 is God's Word, and, like all other Scripture, it is profitable (II Timothy 3:16) and blessed. Indeed, Revelation makes big promises and threatens big curses: if you read it and heed it, you will be blessed, but if you add to it or subtract, you will be cursed (22:18-19). Some would, if they could, block out Revelation altogether from the equation; but this is not an option. So we need to consider what the Lord is saying in this passage, for it is a major part of eschatological teaching.

Millennium Defined

The original ancient word for millennium was chiliasm, which comes from the word chilioi, meaning one thousand. Millennium comes from the Latin mille (1,000) and annus (years). Both these words mean the doctrine of the millennium, the belief that Christ will return to reign on earth for 1,000 years. It is also known as the kingdom age to come.

While it is correct that the phrase "1,000 years" is used only in Revelation (six times), the concept of a kingdom ruled by the Messiah comes from the Old Testament. Prophets, priests, sages and kings longed for this era. God made an immutable and unconditional covenant with David (II Samuel 7:11-16) of an everlasting dynasty, sealed with an oath (Psalm 89:3f, 20 -37). When Jerusalem was besieged by the Babylonians and it looked like the City of David and the Throne of David were going to be overthrown, God graciously reaffirmed the Davidic Covenant in Jeremiah 33:19-22.

In the New Testament the Angel Gabriel announces to the Virgin Mary the birth of Christ who God will give the throne of His father David (Luke 1:32), reigning over the house of Jacob forever (v. 33). Matthew and Luke both give detailed genealogies of Jesus via King David. Since God is faithful to fulfill His promises, literally and physically, the time will come when the "kingdoms of this world" become the "kingdoms of Our Lord and of His Christ, and He shall reign forever and ever!" (Revelation 11:15).

If Matthew 25:31-46; Luke 19:12-15, and Revelation 19:11-20:6 are literally to come to pass, then Jesus Christ is returning to this planet to set up a kingdom, and to sit down on His throne (Matthew 19:28; 25:31; Revelation 3:21). This was the expectation of the twelve apostles: the sons of Zebedee expected this kingdom (Matthew 20:20-24); questions of <u>when</u>, not <u>if</u>, there would be a kingdom were addressed to Jesus just before His Ascension (Acts 1:6f). The Apostle Peter spoke that all things will be restored when Jesus Christ returns to earth (Acts 3:19-21).

This concept seemed simple enough, and indeed, the early church believed in a literal Kingdom/Millennium. However, the transition between the Hebraic and Hellenistic worldview would result in two radically different interpretations of the Millennium.

The Hebraic Worldview is based on covenant, relationship, and is concrete and practical. It uses simple, even daily, illustrations to convey spiritual truth, like the parables of Jesus. The Hebrews are very theo-centric or God-centered. Knowledge starts and ends with God. Thus God-emanating knowledge was, and still is, highly valued with the goal of knowing and serving God, along with learning how to live in this world. There is no duality in the Hebrew mindset but a dynamic body-soul unity.

The Hellenistic mindset is more theoretical, abstract, philosophical, and allegorical, with a more anthro-centric (man-centered) viewpoint, seeking knowledge for knowledge's sake. While Jews put emphasis on functions, Hellenists looked to structure and appearance. Hellenism, thanks to Plato, taught dualism, where the visible material world is inferior and evil, while the invisible spiritual world is desirable and perfect.

Hebraic versus Hellenistic Mindset	
Hebraic Worldview	**Hellenistic Worldview**
Based on covenant	Based on knowledge (gnosis)
Relationship with God	Knowledge of God
Adoption by God	Less familial
Concrete	Abstract
Practical	Theoretical
Theo-centric	Anthro-centric
Monotheistic	Polytheistic
Emphasized inner & outer man	Emphasized outer man
Knowledge is Wholistic	Knowledge for Knowledge's Sake
Functional	Form & Appearance
Dynamic partnership between visible and invisible, body & soul	Dualistic: visible is evil, spiritual is good
Interpretation: Literal	Interpretation: Allegorical

Knowing these worldviews will help us understand why there are such radical interpretations to the Kingdom/Millennial passages. The Church has actually benefited from both mindsets, especially when you consider that Hellenism gave us our Greek New Testament, canon of Scripture, creeds, and church councils. But this God-fearing, Bible-based Hellenism collided with a rabidly polytheistic and seductive Hellenism; a Hellenism that was a challenge to ancient Jews and Christians. The bodily resurrection and Millennium are a Hebraic, not a Hellenistic notion. The idea of living in a physical, though glorified, body on this material earth is offensive to Hellenistic sensitivities.

The following are the major millennial theories: Postmillennialism, Amillennialism, and Premillennialism.

Postmillennialism

The belief that as the Gospel goes forth, the world will become a better place for a thousand years, after which Christ will return and take His people into eternity.

Postmillennialism is the youngest of the major millennial theories, a product of the seventeenth century rationalistic revolution. The Reformation did not concern itself with eschatology, but once Protestantism was established and the Enlightenment came into being, then there was a fresh look at issues like the millennium. Post-Reformation covenant theologians like this view because it offered an alternate view to the Roman Catholics and also fit well with the current rationalistic environment.

The Enlightenment and Industrial Revolution gave the West confidence that it could build a better quality of life—a kingdom of God on earth. The more the Gospel spreads, the more the world becomes Christianized and the better things become. Postmillennialism was the catalyst for the great missionary endeavours of the eighteenth and nineteenth centuries. With the imperial growth of Britain and the United States, postmillennialism was seen as the logical view compatible with a changing world. It is said that by 1901, the Protestant world was firmly postmillennial.

Postmillennialism espouses the spreading of the Gospel, the improvement of society, and hence a "Christianized World" for one thousand years. Until now, this period has yet to commence. But when it comes, it will be completely on earth, politically based, and recognized by both believers and unbelievers.

Like amillennialism, it sees Christ coming after the "millennium" and ushering believers into the Eternal State. Like classic premillennialism, it believes in a literal thousand year golden age on earth but without Christ's physical presence.

The notion that the world was getting better took a mighty battering when the Titanic sunk on its maiden voyage in 1912, and then the First World War broke out two years later, resulting in millions of death. A few months later, the Spanish flu pandemic broke out with even multiple millions more perishing. These terrible shakings caused postmillennialism to rapidly decline. Many abandoned this theory and went to amillennialism.

Decades later postmillennialism made a resurgence through Dominion theologians and Kingdom Now proponents, like Gary North, David Chilton, Rousas Rushdoony, Earl Paulk, and others. As the Gospel spreads, it brings dominion, improved standards, and other millennial conditions, with much of the world being converted.

Postmillennialism

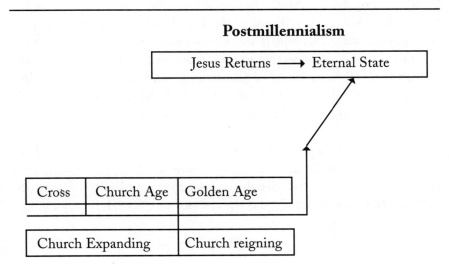

Amillennialism

Amillennialism teaches that the expansion of God's Kingdom during the church age is the "realized millennium," and when Christ returns there will be no literal thousand year reign on earth. Instead, there will be the general resurrection, general judgement, and the redeemed will be ushered immediately into the Eternal State.

This is the second of the great millennial theories. It was not part of early church theology, but had its birth in the fourth century A.D. At that time the church was no longer persecuted by the Roman Empire but, instead, was quickly becoming the state religion. Also, Greek philosophers like Plato, with their dualistic worldview of the material realm being evil and the invisible realm being good, had been "baptized" into Christendom and their philosophies integrated into theology. So a literal, physical millennium was considered inferior to the victorious, triumphant spiritual millennium that was manifest. Remember that our eschatology can be greatly affected by our historical times. With the rise of Christian Constantinople in the fourth century A.D., the "Rome of the East," with its imperial splendour and magnificent cathedrals, it was easy to imagine that one was in the millennium now. Imagine that the once-despised Christian church now converted the Roman Emperor Constantine, and was quickly spreading throughout the empire—surely the spread of the church meant God's Kingdom was here now, a "realized millennium."

Some amillennialists prefer the term "inaugural eschatology" to "realized millennium" because it leaves room for future prophetic fulfillment. They teach that Christ won the decisive victory over sin, death, hell, and the devil, at His Cross. "It is finished" and the victory is final. It is only a matter of time before this wonderful victory is consummated. God's Kingdom is both present (e.g. Luke 17:20-21 *"The Kingdom of God is in the midst of you;* also Rom 14:17; I Cor. 4:19-20; Col. 1:13-14) and future (Mt 7:21-23; 8:11-12; I Cor 6:9; Gal 5:21; Eph. 5:5, 2 Tim 4:18). The "last days" are also future but present (I Jn 2:18; I Cor 10:11; Acts 2:16-17). Regarding Revelation 20, amillennialists say we are in the Millennium now: the Gospel is spreading, Satan is bound and cannot stop the spread of the kingdom, and the saints in Christ are ruling and reigning in heaven.

Amillennialism does believe in future eschatological events, like universal spread of the Gospel, a great apostasy, the great tribulation, coming of antichrist, and the conversion of Israel. While many of these events are not new, they will have an intense and climatic fulfilment in the last days.

Amillennialism is a simple eschatology. When Jesus Christ returns to earth, it will be a single coming, not a rapture and a second coming. There will be a general resurrection of believers and unbelievers, while those believers who were alive at the return of Christ will have glorified bodies (I Cor 15:51-52). Then comes the Judgement Day, which does not determine people's final destiny—a fate already determined—but to show God's glory, the contrast between believers and unbelievers, and then grant rewards or punishments by degree. After the final judgement, the New Jerusalem and the new heaven and earth merge together, and believers enter into the Eternal State. Prophecies consigned to the Millennium will actually be fulfilled in Eternity.

Amillennialism is the millennial theory of choice by many scholars. It is widely embraced by Catholics and Protestants, liberals and conservatives. Because the Protestant reformers endorsed it, there is the stamp of credibility and orthodoxy. Ice & Demy comment:

It is no exaggeration to say that among the church's leadership (including the majority of Protestant reformers during the fifteenth and sixteenth centuries) amillennialism has been the most widely held view for much of the church's history.[2]

Prominent Amillennialist Anthony Hoekema says that if Revelation is written chronologically and its fulfilment is in the future, then "We are then virtually compelled to believe that the thousand-year reign depicted in 20:4 must come after the return of Christ described in 19:11".[3] Hoekema believes that Revelation describes events taking place during the whole of church history, and uses a system of interpretation called "progressive parallelism." This means Revelation has seven sections that run parallel to each other from the time of Christ's first advent to His second.[4]

With the demise of the first phase of postmillennialism during World War I, many turned to amillennialism, rather than premillennialism. A superficial parallel exists between amillennialism and postmillennialism, in that both believe Christ will return after the Millennium. The difference is that postmillennialists believe the world will get better, and the amillennialists say it will not.

---

[2] Thomas Ice & Timothy Demy, *Fast Facts on Bible Prophecy*, Eugene OR: Harvest House Publishers, 1997, page 13.

[3] Anthony Hoekema, "Amillennialism," *The Meaning of the Millennium: Four Views*, edited by Robert G. Clouse; Downer's Grove IL: Intervarsity Press, 1977, page 156.

[4] Progressive Parallelism is defended by William Hendricksen in his commentary on Revelation, called *More than Conquerors*.

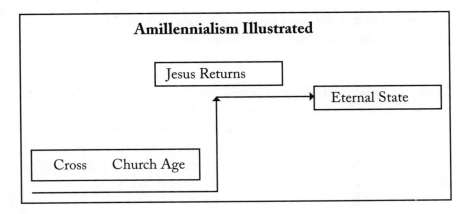

Premillennialism

Upon the return of Jesus Christ to earth, He will set up His kingdom and rule the world for one thousand years from Jerusalem. It literally means that Christ will return to earth before the thousand years.

Premillennialism, like the pre-tribulation rapture theory, is the most literal of the three millennial theories. It was the chosen theory of the early church. Justin Martyr suggested that those who did not believe in it were heretics. Other premillennialists included Barnabas, Hermas, Ignatius, Polycarp, Irenaeus, Justin Martyr, Tertullian, Hippolytus, and Methodius. Origen was the first known theologian to deviate from premillennialism.

Church Historian Philip Schaff says:

The most striking point in the eschatology of the ante-Nicene Age is the prominent chiliasm, or millenarianism, that is the belief in the visible reign of Christ in glory on earth with the risen saints for a thousand years, before the general resurrection and judgement. It was indeed not the doctrine of the church embodied in any creed or form of devotion, but a widely current opinion of distinguished teachers.[5]

With the advent of fourth century amillennialism, premillennialism appeared to be in retreat. Not only was Augustine amillennial, but so was the church historian Eusebius and Bible translator Jerome. For at least thirteen hundred years afterwards, while amillennialism reigned, eschatology in general languished. Very little emphasis was put on Biblical prophecy during this period. Dr. Barry Chant comments:

> In fact, for centuries, there seems to be little evidence of any substantial teaching at all on eschatology, and certainly, virtually nothing of a literal or premillennial flavour.[6]

After the Reformation, when the Bible was available in the language of the vernacular to the average person, interest slowly grew again to prophecy, literal fulfilment, and the Millennium. The Waldenses, Lollards, Wycliffites, some Anabaptists, Sir Isaac Newton, and some Anglican bishops became premillennialists. In the twentieth century, prominent premillennialists included Francis Shaeffer, Carl Henry, George Eldon Ladd, and Merrill Tenney.

In the 19th Century, John Nelson Darby founded the Plymouth Brethren and systematized the teaching of dispensationalism, where all of divine history is divided into seven dispensations or ages. While God Himself does not change, the way He treats Israel and humanity is according to the dispensation (e.g. Dispensation of law requires the stoning of adulterers

---

[5] History of the Christian Church, vol. 2, p. 614, found in Ice Demy [Fast Facts] 1997: 153.

[6] Barry Chant & Winkie Pratney, The Return, Chicester UK: Sovereign World, 1991, page 211.

but the Dispensation of grace means preaching the Gospel to them). The Millennium is the seventh dispensation.

Dispensationalism adopted the old classic premillennialism, except that it put the rapture of the church before the Tribulation, rather than after. With the establishment of modern Israel in 1948, premillennialism made a powerful comeback. After all, if the prophecy of the return of the Jews to Palestine were fulfilled literally, then so will the promises of the coming millennial kingdom. With Israel's conquest and annexation of the Old City of Jerusalem in June 1967, premillennialism was at fever pitch. With the publication of the bestseller, *The Late, Great Planet Earth* by Hal Lindsey three years later, literal interpretation became popularized and widespread, and premillennialism benefited from this.

Premillennialism believes that Christ will return to earth physically, literally, personally and before the Millennium, to set up His Kingdom. When He returns, every eye shall see Him, the dead will hear His voice and rise while the surviving saints will receive transformed, glorified bodies. After destroying the beast (antichrist) and the false prophet, He will sit on His throne in Jerusalem and judge the nations (Matthew 25).

Historic or Classic Premillennialism

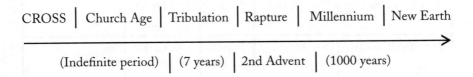

CROSS | Church Age | Tribulation | Rapture | Millennium | New Earth

(Indefinite period) | (7 years) | 2nd Advent | (1000 years)

Dispensational Premillennialism

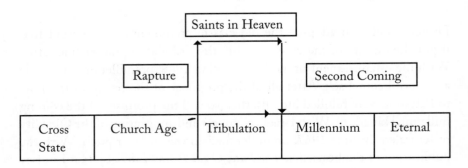

In choosing a millennial view, one needs to ask the big question:

"Is there a literal millennium for Israel in the future **or** are the millennial promises fulfilled for the church **now**, either in heaven or on earth?"

Answer this and you will immediately default to one of the three millennial positions:

The Big Millennial Question				
Theory	For Whom?	When	Where	Rev 20 Literal?
Postmillennialism	The Church	Now	On Earth	No
Amillennialism	The Church	Now	In Heaven & Earth	No
Premillennialism	(Redeemed) Israel & the Church	Future	On Earth	Yes

Here is another way to look at it: put a new Christian in a room with a Bible for thirty days. Ask him or her that when Christ comes again to the earth, will He rule for 1,000 years on earth? Or will He simply take us into the Eternal State? What answer do you think this new Christian will give, without any outside influence? Will he or she emerge postmillennial, amillennial, or premillenial?

REVIEW QUESTIONS:

1. Give a simplified definition of the millennium.
2. Which millennial theory was held by the early church?
3. Which is the preferred theory of scholars?
4. Which was the primary millennial theory of Protestantism around 1900?
5. Which millennial theory is the simplest?
6. Which millennial theory is the most literal?

Part Four

Prophetic Passages

Chapter Nine

Prophetic Passages: Gog & Magog (Ezekiel 38 & 39)

Ezekiel 38:2
2 "Son of man, set your face against Gog, of the land of Magog, the prince of Rosh, Meshech, and Tubal, and prophesy against him,

2 Peter 1:19
19 And so we have the prophetic word confirmed, which you do well to heed as a light that shines in a dark place, until the day dawns and the morning star rises in your hearts;

Matthew Henry's Commentary of Ezekiel 38

"This chapter, and that which follows it, are concerning Gog and Magog, a powerful enemy to the people of Israel, that should make a formidable descent upon them, and put them into a consternation, but their army should be routed and their design defeated; and this prophecy, it is most probable, had its accomplishment some time after the return of the people of Israel out of their captivity, whether in the struggles they had with the kings of Syria, especially Antiochus Epiphanes, or perhaps in some other way not recorded, we cannot tell. If the sacred history of the Old Testament had reached as far as the prophecy, we should have been better able to understand these chapters, but, for want of that key, we are locked out of the meaning of them."[1]

---

[1] Henry, Matthew, *Matthew Henry's Commentary on the Bible*, (Peabody, MA: Hendrickson Publishers) 1997.

145

Introducing Gog and Magog

This remarkable prophetic passage, found in Ezekiel 38 and 39 (after the famous Valley of Dry Bones in chapter 37), speaks about a massive coalition invasion of Israel from the North in the latter days, so overwhelming and unexpected that the only way the nation survives is through manifest divine intervention. It is a remarkable prophecy for its detail, description, and final destiny.

Matthew Henry, writing in 1712, was totally at a loss as to ascribing timing for the fulfillment of this prophecy. He was offering only a guess. One option that did not occur to him is that the prophecy could have a future end-time fulfillment. Even one hundred years ago, scholars would have probably come up with the same conclusion as Henry. But the earth-shaking changes that have happened in the geo-political world since the end of World War II and the Cold War mean that today, virtually all the major ingredients for fulfillment of this prophecy are already in the cupboard, waiting to be mixed and baked.

Gog means "roof, top" and maybe even mountain. Magog simply means "from Gog," so Gog and Magog refers to "Gog from the land of Gog." Gog represents anti-God and anti-Christ forces which are violent in their antagonism to the Word of God and the people of God. Let us look at this prophecy in detail.

Gog & Magog Step-By-Step

1. **It will be in the latter days:** Ezekiel 38:8 (also verse 16) *"After many days you will be visited. In the latter years you will come into the land....*

This seems to be clear enough: the invasion will happen in the latter days (verse 16) or years (verse 2), probably the end of this age. But the big question is "when":

a) Before the Great Tribulation?
b) In the middle of the Tribulation?
c) The end of the Tribulation, namely Armageddon?
d) After the millennium (Rev. 20:8)?

Bear in mind that as you look at the details of this prophecy, all the ingredients are present today. As such, it could very well have a pre-tribulation fulfillment, as affirm some Hebrew Christian scholars like Arnold Fruchtenbaum and Lance Lambert. The fact that there is no mention of the Messiah in this passage lends credence to this view.

2. **The enemy will come from "the far north":** *"... from the far north and all its troops—many people are with you" (38:6); "Then you will come from your place out of the far north, you and many peoples with you..." (38:15); "and I will turn you around and lead you on, bringing you up from the far north, and bring you against the mountains of Israel"* (39:2). The phrase is literally the "uttermost parts of the north." Before 1991, the overwhelmingly unanimous interpretation of this was the Soviet Union, which was a tailor-made villain for a Gog-like invasion. Today the Russian Federation is the successor state of the once-powerful Soviet Union, and the state of its economy and military seems to preclude this kind of armed adventure.

Vladimir Zhironovsky, an ultra-nationalist founder and leader of the Liberal Democratic Party of Russia (LDPR), and a prominent member of Russia's national parliament, The Duma, wrote a provocatively titled book called "The Last Dash to the South," where he wrote about an invasion of Russia's southern Muslim neighbors in order to achieve long-lasting peace. Eqbal Ahmad wrote the following in "*Russia's Tormented Soul*":

> The purpose of the "last thrust" (also known as "The Last Dash to the South), says Vladimir Zhirinovsky is "to liberate the world from war which always begins in the South." He invokes the threat to the western world "from the direction of Teheran which is constructing plans for the pan-Islamic seizure of vast territories, from the direction of Ankara where plans for a greater Turkic state were prepared long ago." He believes that "Russia's true and historic role and destiny is to protect Christianity from the Muslim threat." He would proceed with mission moderately, step by step: first reconquer and abolish the Central Asian republics; then conquer the region from "Karachi to Constantinople." One should note Zhirinovsky's ultimate dreams: "I dream of the day when Russian soldiers can wash their boots in the warm waters of the Indian Ocean." The objective, of course, is peace: "The sound of the bells of Russian Orthodox churches on the shores of the Indian Ocean and the Mediterranean will bring peace to those people." Mr. Zhirinovsky hopes the U.S. would see the advantage in sharing the world with a re-vitalized Russia.[2]

Zhirinovsky does not appear to speak about an attack specifically aimed at Israel. While he may not represent the Russian political mainstream, his nationalist and religious messianism resonates with some Russians and can certainly help contribute to a climate that brings strong militaristic impulses

---

[2] Eqbal Ahmad, *Russia's Tormented Soul*, http://www.geocities.com/CollegePark/Library/9803/eqbal_ahmad/eacol294.html, Accessed 26 April 2006.

But remember that Gog works in coalition, not on its own. Also, Russian Christians greatly dislike the interpretation of Russia equals Gog. They nominate another northern power: China. And China, they add, is still communist!

3. **Israel the People shall be living in the land of Israel at the time of the invasion:** "*After many days you will be visited. In the latter years you will come into the land of those brought back from the sword and gathered from many people on the mountains of Israel....* (38:8) "*Therefore, son of man, prophesy and say to Gog, 'Thus says the Lord GOD: "On that day when My people Israel dwell safely, will you not know it?* (38:14). The remarkable thing is that Ezekiel was writing from exile when most of his people no longer lived in the land. In faith he saw that one day the Jews would return to the land, not as Israel and Judah but as one nation (see chapter 37). "*...against a people gathered from the nations...*" (38:12) shows that this re-gathered Israel will not just return from the Babylonian captivity, but from the global Diaspora it has endured since the time of the destruction of the Second Temple in A.D. 70. Migrants to modern Israel come from over one hundred different nations.

4. **The Gog coalition does not invade willingly:** "*I will turn you around, put hooks into your jaws, and lead you out...*" (38:4). During the Cold War and even until now, most nation states including the great powers, are not rubbing their hands in great anticipation of an invasion, especially against Israel, which has been among the top ten (even five) military powers in the world. Operation Samson, for example, means that a successful Arab-Iranian invasion of Israel will be met with lightning fast nuclear retribution on the major cities of the Middle East. What the prophecy says is that God will put a

hook in Gog's jaw and lead him out. You do not put hooks in domestic animals, which could cause great pain and infection. Hooks are reserved for those animals that are slated for destruction.

5. **The Gog Confederacy is highly armed:** "*...with all your army, horses, and horsemen, all splendidly clothed, a great company with bucklers and shields, all of them handling swords* (38:4)." Probably no area of the world is arming more rapidly than Asia: East Asia, South Asia, China, Russia and the Middle East. While other regions are demilitarizing, this continent is not. It would not be an exaggeration to call some areas an arsenal.

References to horses could be symbolic, but remember that horses can be used in steep and mountainous areas were mechanized forces cannot reach. In October 1917, the Australian Light Horsemen captured the city of Beersheba from the Ottoman Turks, thus spelling the end of four hundred years of Turkish rule in Palestine. In any case, the Muslim world and Russia have enjoyed great cooperation for many decades. Israel has no lack of enemies from this part of the world and the possibility of long-term peace is dim. As Joseph d'Courcy, a renowned intelligence expert says, "The Arabs do not—and never will—accept Israel's right to exist."

6. **The Invasion Force will be as numerous as a cloud that covers the land:** "*You will come up against My people Israel like a cloud, to cover the land*" (38:16). Gog, in concert with its allies, will be so numerous as the cause a blackout. Gog will be a massive and well-aimed bowling ball with Israel as the sole pin in the alley.

7. **The allies of Gog are recent and present day antagonists of Israel:**
"Persia, Ethiopia, and Libya are with them, all of them with shield and helmet. 6 "Gomer and all its troops; the house of Togarmah from the far north and all its troops—many people are with you (38:5-6). Persia is clearly Iran. Historically, it was kind to the Jews like in the days of Cyrus the Great, or murderously hostile like in the time of Haman. During the time of the Shah, there were strong and friendly bilateral ties, but after the establishment of the Islamic Republic of Iran in 1979, Israel now had a new and major enemy. Ethiopia as "Cush" may also mean Sudan, Libya is Phut, Gomer may mean the people north of the Black Sea, and Beth Togarmah can be in the Caucasus Mountains. Some commentators suggest Turkey could enter into the fray; Turkey is a Muslim country but it is has strong relations with Israel. A major tilt towards Islamism, fuelled by a European Union rejection of Turkey's EU membership application, would totally change the balance of power in the Middle East.

8. **What is the purpose of this invasion:** 12 *"to take plunder and to take booty, to stretch out your hand against the waste places that are again inhabited, and against a people gathered from the nations, who have acquired livestock and goods, who dwell in the midst of the land.13 "Sheba, Dedan, the merchants of Tarshish, and all their young lions will say to you, 'Have you come to take plunder? Have you gathered your army to take booty, to carry away silver and gold, to take away livestock and goods, to take great plunder?'* " (38:12-13). Why is the massive and unprovoked invasion occurring? The apparent reason is spoils. It is not clear what spoils Israel could offer the invading Gog. "Livestock and goods" could refer to its successful agricultural sector. The Dead Sea has forty-five billion tons of sodium, chlorine, sulphur, potassium, calcium, magnesium,

and bromide[3]. Though Israel has no oil of its own, its proximity to Middle Eastern oil, which is has seventy percent of the world's proven oil reserves, could make it a strategic toehold for oil and as the Afro-Eurasian land bridge. "Sheba and Dedan" could refer to modern Saudi Arabia and "merchants of Tarshish" may be Lebanon, whose forebears, the Phoenicians, were the great ancient maritime people.

9. **This confrontation will be on the mountains of Israel:** 2 *"and I will turn you around and lead you on, bringing you up from the far north, and bring you against the mountains of Israel"* (39:2). What does this phrase mean? Israel/Palestine is a very small but geographically diverse entity: moon-like deserts in the south, sand dunes on the coast, snow capped mountain in the north, Great Rift Valley on the east, and the Central Hill Country in the middle. One plausible explanation is that these mountains represent the Central Hill Country in the middle, also known as Judea and Samaria or the West Bank. Contained therein are Biblical cities like Shechem (now Nablus), Hebron, Bethlehem, and the big prize of Jerusalem.

10. **Nations beyond the Middle East are involved:** *"And I will send fire on Magog and on those who live in security in the coastlands. Then they shall know that I am the LORD* (39:6). Coastlands can also mean the "isles," like those of the Aegean Islands of Greece, and areas west of Israel, like Europe. International links to Israel/Palestine are nothing new, but today this region dominates world attention like no other. It has been said that one-third of all United Nations resolutions from 1945-1990 were devoted to Israel, Palestine, and Jerusalem. Chuck Missler has commented that the late lights of all major western foreign ministries are burning over the question of Israel and

---

[3] Arnold Fructhenbaum, *The Footsteps of the Messiah*, Tustin CA: Ariel Press, 1990, page 72.

Jerusalem. Zechariah 12:3 says Jerusalem will be the unmovable rock for "all nations" and anyone who tries to move it will injure themselves. The international chaos following a Gog-like invasion is completely plausible.

11. **This force will be divinely destroyed:** 38:18 *"And it will come to pass at the same time, when Gog comes against the land of Israel," says the Lord GOD, "that My fury will show in My face.19 "For in My jealousy and in the fire of My wrath I have spoken: 'Surely in that day there shall be a great earthquake in the land of Israel,22 "And I will bring him to judgment with pestilence and bloodshed; I will rain down on him, on his troops, and on the many peoples who are with him, flooding rain, great hailstones, fire, and brimstone.39:3 "Then I will knock the bow out of your left hand, and cause the arrows to fall out of your right hand.4 "You shall fall upon the mountains of Israel, you and all your troops and the peoples who are with you; I will give you to birds of prey of every sort and to the beasts of the field to be devoured. Ezekiel 38:18, 19, 22; 39:3, 4.* God directly intervenes to defeat the invasion force. So overwhelming is this divine counterattack that it takes Israel seven months to bury the dead (39:12) and seven years worth of fuel will be provided from Gog's arsenal (39:10). Why seven months? Could it be an earthquake, like the rabbis and some Christian teach? The problem is that plagues could break out. Bodies can not be touched but a marker will be set up and then another squad will bury the dead in one of the valleys, perhaps near Amman. Once complete, the valley will be forever sealed and a new city named Hamonah will be set up as a memorial. Some have suggested nuclear, but Lance Lambert tells of a group of nuclear scientists who have suggested chemical and bacteriological destruction.

12. **At the conclusion of this invasion there will be a final regathering of the Jews to Israel:** 27 ' *When I have brought them back from the peoples and gathered them out of their enemies' lands, and I am hallowed in them in the sight of many nations,28 'then they shall know that I am the LORD their God, who sent them into captivity among the nations, but also brought them back to their land, and left none of them captive any longer"* (39:27-28). Something like thirty-seven percent of the world's fourteen million Jews currently live in Israel, but forty-six percent live in North America and twelve percent in Europe. Anti-semitism is rising again in Europe and after the Gog scenario; there will be an influx of Jews to Israel greater than anything that has ever seen before.

13. **The Holy Spirit will be poured out on the Jewish people:** *'And I will not hide My face from them anymore; for I shall have poured out My Spirit on the house of Israel,' says the Lord GOD"* (39:29; also see 37:14 and Joel 2:28-29). Psalm 118:5 says that when you call upon God in your distress, He will answer and set you in a broad place. This seems to be what happens to Israel, spiritually-speaking: regathered and Spirit-filled. It is the fulfillment of what the prophets spoke. Like travail before the joy of birth and tribulation before a millennium, so Gog and Magog usher in some of Israel's major prophetic fulfillments.

14. **Possible hindrance to immediate fulfillment:** *"You will say, 'I will go up against a land of unwalled villages; I will go to a peaceful people, who dwell safely, all of them dwelling without walls, and having neither bars nor gates'* (38:11). Some say that Israel is not living in peace and hence is a fortress, with barbed-wire fences and minefields along the border. A look at its northern most city of Metullah will give you an idea. If this the correct interpretation, then the invasion cannot happen at this

time. Perhaps after a short and savage war, like the one described in Psalm 83 which has not yet happened, may result in the neutralizing of Israel's immediate enemies and thus allow it to relax its military preparedness: dismantling the fortified war borders and erecting peaceful ones. Of interest is not one Arab nation bordering Israel is mentioned as participating in the Gog invasion of Israel. Then the warning of I Thessalonians 5:3 regarding "peace and safety" preceding sudden destruction will come to pass, namely Gog and Magog. Arnold Fruchtenbaum takes a different view when he says that "unwalled villages" is a good description of modern Israeli kibbutzim (agricultural communities) and adds:

"...nowhere in the entire text does it speak of Israel as living in peace. Rather Israel is merely living in security which means "confidence," regardless of whether it is during a state of war or peace".[4]

When you understand the grand sweep of this prophecy and see that its details have only been fulfilled in our day – and miraculously so- then this should make even the most casual observer sit up and take notice. We have a more sure word of prophecy!

REVIEW QUESTIONS:

1. Who is the invasion force?
2. Who is the object of the invasion?
3. What is the motive?
4. What happens to the invasion force after it arrives at its destination?

---

[4] Fruchtenbaum, *ibid*, page 77.

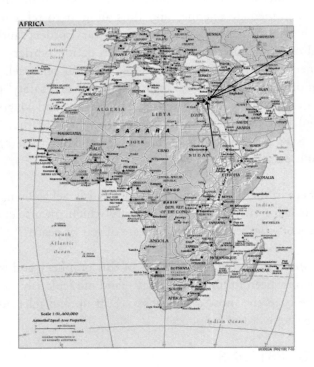

GOG & MAGOG INVASION
(Map Courtesy of the CIA)

Chapter Ten

Prophetic Passages: Matthew 24 and the Olivet Discourse

There could be no more pertinent question to an end-time believer than "when will Jesus return?" For in His return, many things will be realized:

1. We will be with the Lord forever;
2. He will overcome and vanquish all foes;
3. The promises of God will be realized;
4. Christ will establish the Kingdom of God;
5. God's presence and Eternity will be our true home—forever and ever.

Though this question is important for this time, it is not a new one. In fact, it was asked two thousand years ago by those very people who were closest to Jesus, earthly speaking. In order to understand the nature of the last days and the return of Jesus Christ, particularly from the New Testament point-of-view, you cannot go past what is called "The Olivet Discourse." It is found in the three synoptic Gospels: Matthew 24 to 25, Mark 13, and Luke 21:5-36.

What is the "Olivet Discourse?" A "discourse" is usually an extended, and interactive, communication on a specific topic or a speech of a religious nature. The Gospel of John is replete with Christ's discourses: new birth, well of life, Son of God, bread of life, light of the world, the door, good shepherd, etc., all used to build the case that Jesus is both Messiah/Christ and Son of God. "Olivet" refers to the Mount of Olives, just east of Jerusalem on the opposite side to the Kidron Valley. It was here that Jesus gave this discourse to the twelve disciples after His last public encounter with the Jewish leadership at the Temple precincts.

The Olivet Discourse was given by Jesus in response to three questions asked by His disciples in Matthew 24:3:

1. **"Tell us, when will these things be?"** What things? In verses one and two, Jesus speaks about the future destruction of the Temple.

2. **"And what will be the sign of Your coming..."** The usual understanding of this question concerns the second coming of Christ, not the rapture. The former will be preceded by sign(s) but the latter can happen at any time; this is called the doctrine of imminence.

3. **"And what will be the sign ... of the end of the age"** (sometimes translated "end of the world," for though the earth abides for ever, the world system does not).

In order to obtain answers to these three questions, it is important that the Olivet Discourse is viewed from the perspective of all three Gospels. Each has details that the others do not have.

For our purposes, we will look at a portion of Matthew 24 to see if we can answer a crucial question: was this passage already fulfilled or does it have a future fulfilment. In short, is Matthew 24 history or prophecy?

Putting the Olivet Discourse in Context

Jesus spoke the Olivet Discourse just after His condemnation of the Pharisees (23:13-36) and lamentation over Jerusalem (23:37-39). From this point forward, Jesus would have no further public ministry in Israel, since the discourse is spoken two days before His death (Matthew 26:1-2).

One key issue is: to whom is Jesus speaking? Is it to the New Testament church or to Israel? In order to have a proper understanding of what the Lord is saying in this crucial Scripture, let us remember:

1. Jesus is characterizing and condemning the Pharisees, an ancient sect of Biblical Judaism, the predecessor of today's Rabbinic Judaism;

2. Jesus is lamenting over the City of Jerusalem. At that time Jerusalem was the centre of Jewish political and religious life, particularly with the centrepiece being Herod's Temple. Jerusalem is rightly accused of:

A. Killing the prophets and messengers.

B. Refusing to let Messiah gather her children.

C. As a result, "your house" (v. 38) will be left to you desolate. This means that the Temple, the center of Jewish life, will be destroyed. How remarkable? Earlier in His ministry Jesus called the Temple "My Father's house" (John 2:16); now it is no longer God's house, but Israel's. Does this mean that God had already left or disowned the Temple? The nuance here is revealing.

D. Jesus the Messiah will not see Israel again ... and for some theologians, this is the end of the story. Israel rejected Messiah, and there will be no further encounter with Him. But the entire sentence says "*...you shall see Me no more till you say, 'Blessed is He who comes in the name of the LORD!'*" (23:39). Popular commentary says that Israel will see the Messiah when they finally invite Him back at their darkest hour. Considering the many dark hours of Jewish history, from Haman to Hitler, this final future period will be the darkest and most dangerous of all. Only the Kingly Messiah has the power and authority to deliver Israel in time of need.

E. Until now, all the issues involved the Jewish people and Jerusalem. Then at the start of chapter 24, Jesus and His disciples are walking out of the Temple compound permanently. He will no longer be teaching there or overturning the money changer's tables. His appointment with Calvary awaits Him.

On their way out, the disciples are admiring the beautiful work of Herod's Temple. Commenced in 20 B.C. by Herod the Great, it was still being completed nearly fifty years later when Jesus spoke these words. Final completion would not occur until A.D. 64, just six years before its destruction by the Romans. Without question, Herod's Temple[1] one of the most impressive buildings of antiquity. Even his most antagonistic

---

[1] It was really God's Temple but Herod was the builder or renovator.

religious foes had to admit, like the rabbinic statement "Whoever has not seen Herod's building has never seen a beautiful building in his life.ⁱ" Yet Jesus, who had just referred to the Temple as "(Israel's) house," says that, "not one stone shall be left here upon another, that shall not be *thrown down*" (24:2).

In summary, it is twelve Jewish disciples asking their Jewish rabbi about issues affecting the Jewish Temple and the end of the current age, the return of the Messiah, and the ushering in of the Messianic age.

Taking a Closer Look

Acts 17:11

11 These (the people of Berea in Macedonia) *were more fair-minded than those in Thessalonica, in that they received the word with all readiness, and searched the Scriptures daily to find out whether these things were so.*

When it comes to Bible study in general or eschatology specifically, it is vital that students look at the Scriptures for themselves. In this section, we are going to take a closer look at Matthew 24 to give some insight into detail. The reader is encouraged to learn inductive Bible study, where one learns to "scuba dive" into the Word rather than merely "snorkel." It is an outstanding method of going deeper into the Word.

Outline of Matthew 24

MATTHEW 24 (NKJV)

15 Therefore when you see the 'abomination of desolation,' spoken of by Daniel the prophet, standing in the holy place" (whoever reads, let him understand), 16 then let those who are in Judea flee to the mountains. 17 Let him who is on the housetop not go down to take anything out of his house. 18 And let him who is in the field not go back to get his clothes. 19 But woe to those who are pregnant and to those who are nursing babies in those days! 20 And pray that your flight may not be in winter or on the Sabbath. 21 For then there will be great tribulation, such as has not been since the beginning of the world until this time, no, nor ever shall be. 22 And unless those days were shortened, no flesh would be saved; but for the elect's sake those days will be shortened. 23 Then if anyone says to you, 'Look, here is the Christ!' or 'There!' do not believe it. 24 For false christs and false prophets will rise and show great signs and wonders to deceive, if possible, even the elect. 25 See, I have told you beforehand. 26 Therefore if they say to you, 'Look, He is in the desert!' do not go out; or 'Look, He is in the inner rooms!' do not believe it. 27 For as the lightning comes from the east and flashes to the west, so also will the coming of the Son of Man be. 28 For wherever the carcass is, there the eagles will be gathered together. 29 Immediately after the tribulation of those days the sun will be darkened, and the moon will not give its light; the stars will fall from heaven, and the powers of the heavens will be shaken. 30 Then the sign of the Son of Man will appear in heaven, and then all the tribes of the earth will mourn, and they will see the Son of Man coming on the clouds of heaven with power and great glory. 31 And He will send His angels with a great sound of a trumpet, and they will gather together His elect from the four winds, from one end of heaven to the other.

Key Words

Tribulation: v. 19, 21 (2x); 22 (2x).
Son of Man: v. 27, 30 (2x), he 31 (3x)
Elect: v. 15 (2x), 16, 17 (21x), 18 (2x), 22, 23, 24, 25, 26, 31
Heaven(s): v. 29, 30 (2x), 31

To Whom Does It Pertain?

The most literal rendering is to the Jewish disciples, as outlined above. What would be the relevance to Gentiles of the Abomination of Desolation (verse 15, only can occur in the Temple), fleeing from Judea (verse 16), the capital territory of Israel, or praying that the flight would not be on the Sabbath (verse 20)?

Action

V. 16 Judeans, flee to mountains
V. 17 Don't return to the house to take
V. 18 Field, don't return for clothes
V. 20 Pray to avoid Sabbath (Jews)

Great Tribulation

V. 15 When you see the Abomination of Desolation[2]
V. 21 Unparalleled trouble
V. 22 Deadly
V. 22 Grace—days will be shortened
V. 23 Deception
V. 24 Falsehood
V. 25 Forewarned
V. 26 Misleading

Second Coming

V. 27 Visible return
V. 28 Death vs. life
V. 29 Blackout
V. 30 Sign in heaven ... tribes mourn ... see Son of man comes.
V. 31 send angels, trumpet, gather Elect four winds, "heaven" to other.

Preterists and some amillennialists and postmillennialists say that Matthew 24 was fulfilled in A.D. 70 and there is no future tribulation.

---

[2] This starts the second half of the Great Tribulation.

Most everyone agrees that the events of A.D. 70, which include the destruction of the Jewish Temple, the end of the Jewish commonwealth in Israel, and the dispersal of the Jews of Israel to the nations (Luke 21:24), have prophetic significance. But if Matthew 24 is history, the question is: when does Christ return? When does the current age end?

The key terms include:

"Abomination of Desolation," (Daniel 9:27; 12:11; Matthew 24:15; Mark 13:14; II Thessalonians 2:3-4; Revelation 13:15). This is the starting point of the second half of the tribulation, where the covenant is broken. Antichrist will move his capital from Babylon to Jerusalem, enter into the Temple of God and declare himself to be god (II Thessalonians 2:3-10).

There is debate whether the term "temple" refers to a literal building in Jerusalem **or** could refer to the body of Christ as the mystical temple. According to *Vine's Expository Dictionary of New Testament Words*, "The weight of Scripture evidence is in favor of the view that it refers to a literal "temple" in Jerusalem, to be reconstructed in the future (cf. Dan. 11:31 and 12:11, with Matt. 24:15)."[ii] After this, the false prophet will set up in the holy of holies an image of the antichrist (Revelation 13:11-15; Daniel 12:11). Whoever does not worship this image will be killed. Israel will be in retreat as anti-semitism rears its ugliest head ever.

"Generation" is mentioned in Matthew 24:34 which says *"Assuredly, I say to you, this generation will by no means pass away till all these things take place."* So what does the term "generation" mean? For some, it means the generation alive in the first century when Jesus spoke these words. Others say it is the generation who is alive when the prophetic signs manifest and will be alive when all is fulfilled. A third option is described by Dwight Pentecost:

...others hold that the word generation is to be taken in its basic usage of race, kindred, family, stock, breed," so that the Lord is here promising that the nation of Israel shall be preserved until the consummation of her program at the second advent in spite of the work of the Desolator to destroy her. This seems to be the best explanation.[3]

Jewish believers' flight: Jesus said that when you see Jerusalem surrounded by armies, then you know its desolation is near (Luke 21:20-24). When the Roman general Cestus Gallus took his army to surround Jerusalem, Jewish believers remembered the words of Jesus. However, they were not permitted to leave because of the Roman siege. Gallus temporarily suspended the siege while he secured his supply lines and the believers took this opportunity to flee to the city of Pella on the eastern side of the Jordan River. Gallus was killed and Vespasian and his son Titus re-started the siege that led to the destruction of the Temple and the city in A.D. 70. For a detailed and possibly eye-witness account, refer to the *Complete Works of Josephus Flavius*, a classic of the first century A.D.

Location of the Second Coming: In Matthew 24:28, there is a strange statement by Christ regarding His coming: "*For wherever the carcass is, there the eagles will be gathered together.*" The KJV uses the term "vultures." Fruchtenbaum makes these comments:

> The body refers to Israel while the vultures refer to the Gentile nations coming against the body of Israel. The place of the second coming of Christ will be in that place where the body of Israel is located, and where the Gentile nations are gathered

---

[3] Dwight Pentecost, *Things to Come*, Grand Rapids: Zondervan, 1964, page 281.

together. The exact place is known as Bozrah in Hebrew, or Petra in Greek. That is where the body will be gathered (Micah 2:12-13), that is where the vultures will come against them (Isaiah 34:1-7, 63:1-6), and that will be the place of the second coming (Habakkuk 3:3).[4]

Though there are some interesting insights here, Fruchtenbaum does not explain why the term "carcass" is used, which normally refers to something that is dead. Israel, in this interpretation, is fighting for its life. Perhaps the implication is that Israel is as good as dead, even when fleeing and hiding in Bozrah, and unless there is divine intervention, the vultures are preparing for a feast.

Nature of the Second Coming: Matthew 24:29-30 speaks of the setting of the Second Coming. It will be preceded by the darkening of the sun, moon, and stars. In other words, a total black out, with the heavenly bodies being shaken. When Christ comes, He will have power and great glory. Glory, here, could refer to the famous Shekinah, a term not used in Scripture but employed by the Jews to describe either a luminous cloud or a brilliant light encased in a cloud. It occurred at Mount Sinai (Exodus 24:9-18), in the holy of holies in the Tabernacle (where the Ark of the Covenant resided) and also that of Solomon's Temple. It is uncertain whether shekinah glory was present in Zerubbabel's and Herod's Temple. New Testament references include Luke 2:9, John 1:14, and Romans 9:4. The Second Coming will certainly be a time of contrasts: when things are at their utter darkest, then will God's light shine brightest.

---

[4] Arnold Fruchtenbaum, *The Footsteps of the Messiah,* Tustin CA: Ariel Press, 1990, page 442.

History or Prophecy?

Could the events of Matthew 24 been fulfilled in history, or are they yet to come? Please consider the following points:

1. **Abomination of Desolation:** 24:15 speaks of the Abomination of Desolation. While Jerusalem was destroyed in A.D. 70, there is no evidence whatsoever of an abomination of desolation. Rome destroyed the Temple but neither Gallus, Vespasian, nor Titus ever entered the Holy of Holies and demanded to be worshipped as God. Josephus does not make any reference to this event. Either the term abomination of desolation is an allegory of the apostasy of the true church, the "temple of the living God," or it has a future fulfilment.

2. **Nature of the Tribulation:** 24:21 *For then there will be great tribulation, such as has not been since the beginning of the world until this time, no, nor ever shall be.* This period will be the most intense the world has ever seen and this could not have been the case in A.D. 70. Certainly, the twentieth century was the most changed filled, cataclysmic, blood-stained period in history. At the dawn of the twenty-first century came the infamous September 11th terrorist attacks and a possible portent of things to come.

3. **Severity of the Tribulation:** Verse 22 says that unless those days are shortened, no flesh shall be saved. Has there ever been a time like this before our time? The possibility of the destruction of all flesh was non-existent until we entered the nuclear age. Now there are other possibilities, like the development of chemical

and bacteriological weaponry. Stockpiled by several key nations, mix these with the long-standing tribal disputes and "hot spots" peppered throughout the world and you have verse 22 becoming plausible for the first time in history.

4. **Coming of Christ:** Everything we have learned so far has been merely the birth pangs of the coming kingdom. The culmination of all these events is the parousia, the visible, personal, bodily return of Jesus Christ. Clearly, the greatest argument in favour of Matthew 24 as prophecy is the fact that Jesus has not yet returned to earth. When He comes, it will be with great glory, every eye shall see Him, He will gather His elect and take full control.

Regardless of your own personal view, is not the coming of the LORD the most important date in your destiny? Even so, echo with the Spirit and the Bride, "Come, Lord Jesus" (Revelation 22:17).

REVIEW QUESTIONS:

1. What do the two key terms "Olivet" and "Discourse" mean?
2. What are the "Jewish aspects" of Matthew 24?
3. Where is the proposed location of the Second Coming, according to Fruchtenbaum?

---

[i] If Herod, who was appointed king of the Jews by the Roman occupiers, and was despised because of his Idumean ethnicity, thought that he could win the love of his Jewish subjects by building the Temple, he was greatly mistaken. One thing he did earn from them: fear and contempt.

[ii] The following is the complete entry out of Vine's:

TEMPLE

1. *hieron* (2411), the neuter of the adjective hieros, "sacred," is used as a noun denoting "a sacred place, a temple," that of Artemis (Diana), Acts 19:27; that in Jerusalem, Mark 11:11, signifying the entire building with its precincts, or some part thereof, as distinct from the naos, "the inner sanctuary" (see No. 2); apart from the Gospels and Acts, it is mentioned only in 1 Cor. 9:13. Christ taught in one of the courts, to which all the people had access. Hieron is never used figuratively. The Temple mentioned in the Gospels and Acts was begun by Herod in 20 B.C., and destroyed by the Romans in A.D. 70.

2. *naos* (3485), "a shrine or sanctuary," was used (a) among the heathen, to denote the shrine containing the idol, Acts 17:24; 19:24 (in the latter, miniatures); (b) among the Jews, the sanctuary in the "Temple," into which only the priests could lawfully enter, e.g., Luke 1:9, 21, 22; Christ, as being of the tribe of Judah, and thus not being a priest while upon the earth (Heb. 7:13, 14; 8:4), did not enter the naos; for 2 Thess. 2:4 see Note (below); (c) by Christ metaphorically, of His own physical body, John 2:19, 21; (d) in apostolic teaching, metaphorically, (1) of the church, the mystical body of Christ, Eph. 2:21; (2) of a local church, 1 Cor. 3:16, 17; 2 Cor. 6:16; (3) of the present body of the individual believer, 1 Cor. 6:19; (4) of the "Temple" seen in visions in the Apocalypse, 3:12; 7:15; 11:19; 14:15, 17; 15:5, 6, 8; 16:1, 17; (5) of the Lord God Almighty and the Lamb, as the "Temple" of the new and heavenly Jerusalem, Rev. 21:22. See SANCTUARY and HOLY, B (b), par. 4.

Notes: (1) The "temple" mentioned in 2 Thess. 2:4 (naos), as the seat of the Man of Sin, has been regarded in different ways. The weight of Scripture evidence is in favor of the view that it refers to a literal "temple" in Jerusalem, to be reconstructed in the future (cf. Dan. 11:31 and 12:11, with Matt. 24:15). For a fuller examination of the passage, see *Notes on Thessalonians,* by Hogg and Vine, pp. 250-252. (2) *For oikos,* rendered "temple," Luke 11:51, KJV, see HOUSE, No. 1. ii

Part Five

Invisible,
Individual Eschatology

Chapter Eleven

Personal or Invisible Eschatology

James Darrow[1], a mild-mannered, likeable guy had just finished his class at the College of the Arts and raced to catch to a Lilydale-bound train in suburban Melbourne, Australia. This is the train he normally catches but he had just missed it. No worries, the next one was just ten minutes later. As he settles down in his seat on the later train, he is busily looking at sheet music; James was a musician and supported his family through gigs and busking. As the train pulled into the Box Hill Station, a stranger comes up to him, and grabs the guitar by James' side. He drops the sheet music, an argument starts, a long knife is produced, and within ten seconds James is struck three times in the chest. The train doors open, the wounded man staggers out of the train with a female passenger, steps on the platform, collapses in a pool of blood, and dies within minutes, while she holds his hand. He was just 28 years old.

This real story, tragic as it is, raises many important questions that are not easy to answer. As for the "why did it happen," one of the key explanations is that we are in a fallen world, where nasty things can and do happen to nice people. The even more important question is the one we barely ask aloud: what happens to James after death? Does he merely "go to sleep" or will he have a conscious existence, either of bliss or torment.

The topic to which we refer is called the "Intermediate State," which is defined as human existence between physical death and physical

---

[1]Name changed though this a real life incident.

resurrection. All people who have ever lived and died are currently in the intermediate state. Since Eschatology is the doctrine of "last things," the state of an individual after their physical death is as much a part of this theology as the Books of Daniel and Revelation. Other ways to refer to it include "personal eschatology" or "invisible eschatology."

Three Types of Death

Death is universally known and feared; it is a formidable foe and an egalitarian reaper, mowing down young, old, rich, poor, black, white, and everyone else under its blade. Its grip is so tight and strong that neither ideology, religion, human resources, or nuclear power, is able to overcome it. The only one who has done so is Jesus Christ, and He promises to help His followers do likewise.

There is much misunderstanding and mythology about the nature of death, as well as the destination of the dead. It is important to stick closely to the Scriptures, for as God's Word, He is the best authority on this last enemy and on its final defeat.

Death is defined as absence of life or the cessation of bodily functions. Some see it as when the heart stops beating or when the person ceases to breathe; however, people in such states have been resuscitated back to life. So what is death? Biblically speaking, death means separation. For example, a divorce is literally the death of a marriage, where a husband and wife legally and permanently separate. Physical death is the separation of the invisible person (soul/spirit) from the visible person (body). The three types of death include:

Spiritual Death

God solemnly warned Adam that on the day he ate of the fruit of the tree of knowledge of good and evil, he would surely die (Gen 2:17). Those familiar with the story know that neither Adam nor Eve dropped dead the moment they ate the forbidden fruit; in fact, they lived on for many years and even bore children. So what kind of death did the first couple experience on the day they sinned? It is called "spiritual death;" separation from God's presence, power, and purity. No longer in close and vibrant union with God, they were evicted from the garden of God and His presence, consigned to living a life of futility, frustration, degeneration, and decay, awaiting physical death. Ephesians 2:1 describes spiritual death this way, *"And you He made alive, who were dead in trespasses and sins."* Spiritual death can only be remedied through salvation in Christ.

Physical Death

This is the death we are all familiar with. This is when the soul/spirit separates from the physical body (James 2:26). The dead body is either cremated, tossed into the sea, or buried. As for the soul/spirit, it goes into one of two places: torment or the presence of the Lord in heaven. Physical death is the natural consequence of the spiritual death incurred by Adam and Eve (Romans 5:21; 6:23; 1 Corinthians 15:56). The Bible teaches that death is an enemy, a judgement (Romans 1:32; 5:16), unnatural, and a curse. For the believer, we are no longer to fear death (I Corinthians. 15:55-57); its sting is removed (I Corinthians 15:55-57), and we become absent from the body but present with the Lord (II Corinthians 5:8).

Eternal Death

Hebrews 9:29 says that people will die once and afterwards comes the judgement. If God's one and only solution to spiritual death—namely the Gospel of Jesus Christ—is rejected or ignored, then at the time of physical death the individual becomes a candidate for eternal death. In the intermediate state they will await their final, irreversible judgement and punishment in the lake of fire (Jude 7; Matthew 18:8; 25:41). Other terms include "everlasting destruction" (II Thessalonians 1:9) and "eternal condemnation" (Mark 3:29).

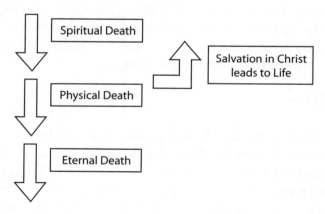

The Intermediate State

19 "There was a certain rich man who was clothed in purple and fine linen and fared sumptuously every day. 20 "But there was a certain beggar named Lazarus, full of sores, who was laid at his gate, 21 "desiring to be fed with the crumbs which fell from the rich man's table. Moreover the dogs came and licked his sores. 22 "So it was that the beggar died, and was carried by the angels to Abraham's bosom. The rich man also died and was buried. 23 "And being in torments in Hades, he lifted up his eyes and saw Abraham afar off, and Lazarus in his bosom.24 "Then he cried and said, 'Father Abraham, have mercy on me, and send Lazarus that he may dip the tip of his finger in water and cool my tongue; for I am tormented in this flame.'25 "But Abraham said, 'Son, remember that in your lifetime you received your good things, and likewise Lazarus evil things; but now he is comforted and you are tormented.26 'And besides all this, between us and you there is a great gulf fixed, so that those who want to pass from here to you cannot, nor can those from there pass to us.'27 "Then he said, 'I beg you therefore, father, that you would send him to my father's house,28 'for I have five brothers, that he may testify to them, lest they also come to this place of torment.'29 'Abraham said to him, 'They have Moses and the prophets; let them hear them.'30 'And he said, 'No, father Abraham; but if one goes to them from the dead, they will repent.'31 "But he said to him, 'If they do not hear Moses and the prophets, neither will they be persuaded though one rise from the dead.' "

From this story we can make the following assertion:

1. **Appointed Place:** The dead go to a place assigned to them by God, depending on their relationship with Him (vs. 22, 23, and 25). They do not roam around at leisure.

2. **Conscious Existence:** The dead have a conscious existence after death. The dead "rich man" has a conversation with an equally dead father Abraham, and is fully aware of his surroundings and circumstances. They are as recognizable in the next world as they were in this one, hence, their current existence continues on thanks to the soul/spirit. In the Transfiguration, Peter easily recognized the persona of Moses and Elijah, though he had never seen them before

and had no physical description of them. Nor were they wearing a name badge!

3.   **Two possible locations:** There were two possible locations for the dead, either a place of bliss (called "Abraham's bosom" and also known as Paradise [Luke 23:43]) or "torments in Hades."

4.   **Fixed Abode:** Once assigned to a place, the dead cannot change location, due to a great chasm separating the two places (v. 26).

5.   **This life determines next:** The end location of the next life is determined by what happens in this one (v. 25).

6.   **Communication with the Living:** The dead apparently do not communicate with the living, and if they would and could, they would warn against the place of torment (v. 28).

7.   **Moses and the Prophets:** The Old Testament was sufficient enough to inform, inspire, and warn people about their eternal destiny. Failure to obey the Scriptures meant that torments would be the intermediate state destination, and even seeing someone rise from the dead will not persuade them, preposterous sounding as this may be (v. 31). This was proven in the Bible; Jesus' Jewish opponents did not accept Moses nor did they change their minds when Christ rose from the dead.

This story is a picture of the intermediate state. As such, neither group of people, the righteous nor unrighteous, will remain in their intermediate location. Since the death and resurrection of Jesus, however, the righteous no longer go to "Abraham's Bosom/Paradise."

Paradise Lost, Heaven Gained

The following explanation is the traditional description about what happens to the dead between the two testaments. It does not answer all questions, but gives us a template from which to study further.

Prior to Christ's redeeming death on the Cross, both the righteous and unrighteous were sent to *sheol* (Hebrew) or *hades* (Greek), which is translated "grave" but also means the underworld of the departed dead. *Sheol/Hades* was partitioned into two parts: Abraham's Bosom, also known as Paradise and the Torments. Satan held the keys of death and hell. The Old Testament sacrificial system appears to have been sufficient to place the righteous in the "paradise compartment" of *sheol*, but was totally inadequate to take them to heaven. Because Christ's blood had not been shed for sin, the righteous dead could not yet dwell in heaven (Leviticus 17:11; Roman 5:8-9; Hebrews 9:22) with a holy God.

When Christ died on the cross, He also descended into Hades for three days and nights (Matthew 12:40, Sheol is in the heart of earth, see Ephesians 4:9, 10; Numbers 16:33). The devil unlocked paradise to let Christ in, to take His place among the righteous dead. Instead, He took the keys of death and hell (Rev. 1:18) off the devil and liberated all the righteous souls, leading them to heaven.[2] He declared His victory over Satan to the righteous (I Peter 3:18-19; 4:6). Ephesians 4:8-10 describes this further (see also II Corinthians 12:1-4).

Today, Abraham's bosom/Paradise is now empty, since believers who die *"depart and be with Christ, which is far better"* (Philippians 1:23), to be *"absent from the body and to be present with the Lord"* (II Corinthians 5:8). The picture we have of these righteous saints is in heaven before

God's throne (Revelation 6:9 and 7:9). On the other hand, the torments section of hades is still inhabited and operative. Frightfully, it admits new occupants every day.

Final Destination

The Righteous

Today the righteous have the promise of God's presence in life (Matthew 28:20) and also in death. They do not lose consciousness (Philippians 1:23), and their soul/spirit goes immediately into the presence of the Lord (II Corinthians 5:8; Philippians 1:21-24; Revelation 6:9-11) bypassing Paradise altogether. At the rapture of the church (I Thessalonians 4:13-18), their soul/spirit is reunited with their glorified body.

Next on the prophetic program is the "Judgement Seat of Christ," where believers will receive rewards for their works (II Corinthians 5:10), rather than the Great White Throne judgement, where unbelievers receive punishment. After this is the Marriage of the Lamb followed by the Marriage Supper of the Lamb (Rev. 19:7-10). Since believers will "ever be with the Lord" (I Thessalonians 4:17), they will follow Him wherever He goes, including Armageddon, the Millennium, or the Eternal State. Ultimately, the righteous will live with God in the New Jerusalem, which will be on earth.

---

[2]There were saints who were resurrected and walked on the earth in Matthew 27:52-53; we do not have any further information about them but it would seem reasonable to assume that they are now with the Lord.

The Unrighteous

The unrighteous dead continue to live in the torments section of hades, as they have all along. This will continue through the tribulation and millennium periods. After the millennium, there will be a general resurrection where the dead will stand before God and face their final destination at the Great White Throne. Revelation 20:13-15 says it all:

> *13 The sea gave up the dead who were in it, and Death and Hades delivered up the dead who were in them. And they were judged, each one according to his works.14 Then Death and Hades were cast into the lake of fire. This is the second death.15 And anyone not found written in the Book of Life was cast into the lake of fire.*

Heaven

Heaven is a real place, where all born again believers have citizenship (Philippians 3:20) and their names are inscribed (Luke 10:20). God and the righteous spirits live there (Hebrews 12:22-24) and is a place of indescribable beauty (see Revelation 4 and the throne of God). However, heaven is the throne of God and earth is His footstool, yet eventually the footstool will be the abode of us all (Revelation 21:2-3).

Hell

As heaven is incomparably wonderful, hell is indescribably horrible. It is everything that heaven is not and lacks all the heaven has to offer. Yet do not think that it is equal in size and capacity to heaven, anymore than the devil is an equal match for God. It is not.

Scripture shows us that hell is:

1. A real place (Luke 16:19);
2. It is where the dead are conscious and in torment (Luke 16:23-28; Deut. 32:22; 2 Sam. 22:6; Isaiah 14:9-11).
3. It is a place without escape (Luke 16:26) or mercy (verse 24).
4. It is located in the "lower parts of the earth" (Psalm 63:9; Matthew 12:40; Ephesians 4:8-10).
5. The "everlasting fire" has been prepared for the devil and his angels (Matthew 25:41) as well as the ungodly who reject Jesus Christ as God (Matthew 8:29; 25:41; Revelation 20:10-15; II Peter 2:4; Jude 6,7
6. Hades and torments will be emptied out at the general resurrection, when the (unrighteous) dead stand before God and are judged according to their works. Those not found in the Book of Life are cast into the lake of fire, where the beast, false prophet, and Satan are (Revelation 19:20; 20:10, 14, 15).

Hell is horrendous; but so are sin and rejecting God's holiness, grace, and love. Our sin-stained minds have little idea of the damage, corruption, and defilement that sin causes on that which God created. Heaven and eternity could never be the pristine pure pinnacle of our existence if God were to tolerate a smidgeon of sin. Death would once again invade life. So sin, death, and hell, have to be treated with the contempt and Godly severity that they truly deserve. People who understand these things become outstanding evangelists.

Remember James Darrow at the beginning of this chapter? There were many tragedies because of his untimely death: he would never been seen by friends or family again in this life (which is very short anyway); he would never watch his son grow up; enjoy the blessings of married life; play the guitar; entertain people; reach his full potential; or be a support to his parents in old age. But all of these tragedies pale into insignificance compared to 'where did he go when he died?'

The truth is: only God knows for sure. But the fact that he had no known commitment to Christ and he was living in a de facto relationship with his girlfriend does not look promising. Yes, he was a pleasant and gentle soul, likeable, a born leader, caring and kind. But these things cannot and will not get one into heaven. For sin is our universal plight and keeps the best of us out (Romans 3:23; 6:23), and only through Jesus Christ becoming Saviour in your life do have your sole opportunity to escape the fires of hell.

False Ideas About the Intermediate State

Cults and false sects have produced all kinds of soothing and misleading notions about the intermediate state. Some of these include:

Soul Sleep
After physical death, the soul simply goes to sleep and quietly awaits the resurrection. It is assumed that the soul cannot function without the body and the Bible calls death "sleep" (John 11:11-14; I Thessalonians 4:13-14). However, it is not the soul that is sleeping, but the body. After all, the rich man, Lazarus, and father Abraham were definitely not asleep. II Corinthians 5:6-8 speaks about "pleasing God" even when we are dead. The question is: how do you please God if you are asleep? People will

either be in torments or heaven before they are judged (Hebrews 9:27).

Annihilationism

The unrighteous dead have no conscious existence after death because they are incinerated. Because of words like "death, perish, destruction" (John 3:16; 8:51; Romans 9:22), it is assumed that the unrighteous will cease to exist. If this is the case, what do we do with the passages that speak about the continued existence and punishment of the unbeliever (Ecclesiastes 12:7; Matthew 25:46; Romans 2:5-10; Revelation 14:11)? Furthermore, the Bible speaks about degrees of punishment (Luke 12:47; Romans 2:12; Revelation 20:12) and this is not possible with annihilationism.

Conditional Immortality

It asserts that the human soul is not created immortal; only God is. Only when a person comes to Jesus Christ, and is resurrected does he or she receive immortality (I Corinthians 15:53). As for the unrighteous, they will be resurrected, judged, punished in the lake of fire proportional to their sins, and then face total destruction/extinction of both body and soul (Matthew 10:28). The key issue here is the immortality of the soul, for if it is not immortal, then this doctrine is correct. Henry Thiessen says:

> Those who hold this position argue that God alone has immortality (I Tim. 6:16), and he gives it to those who respond to his call. They further teach that Scripture nowhere speaks of the immortality of the soul. But we answer that this doctrine confuses immortality with eternal life. The eternal life received at salvation is more than eternal existence;

it is rather a quality of life, a richness of life in the presence of Christ. It is true that God alone has inherent immortality; nevertheless, man did receive derived immortality at creation. He is born as an immortal being.[3]

Purgatory

This is a Roman Catholic and Eastern Orthodox doctrine that teaches that after death the pure souls enter into heaven but the impure believers go to a place of purging of their venial sins. It is not a place of probation and the afflicted soul loses precious time in heaven. Time in purgatory can be reduced by prayers and gifts; it was the selling of indulgences to lessen purgatory time that served as the catalyst for the Protestant Reformation. The sole reference to purgatory is in the apocryphal book of II Maccabees 12:42-45.[i]

Apart from the fact that we are at a loss to find this doctrine in the canon of Scripture, there comes the issue of the sufficiency of Christ's sacrifice for our sins. He paid the price in full and there salvation is by grace through faith (Hebrews 10:1-23; Ephesians 2:8-10; Romans 3:24-28; 5:1,2,9,10; 8:1,31-39; 10:8-11; I John 2:1,2; 3:1,2). While people may suffer temporal punishments for sin in this life, there is nothing in Scripture to indicate that such punishments will continue into the intermediate state.
In summarizing the intermediate state, we return to Thiessen:

We conclude that at death the believer enters into the presence of Christ. He remains with the Lord in a state of conscious blessedness until the time of the resurrection[ii], at which time he will receive his body of glory. The

---

[3]Henry Thiessen, *Lectures in Systematic Theology*, Grand Rapids: William B. Eerdmans, 1989, page 340.

unbeliever enters into a state of conscious torment until the resurrection, at which time he will be cast into the lake of fire. The doctrines of purgatory, soul-sleep, annihilationism, and conditional immortality cannot be considered biblical doctrines.[4]

Which Way Did He Go?

A tombstone in the American state of Ohio symbolizes the issues of the intermediate state and our end-time destiny. It is good ammunition for evangelists:

> Not so fast, stranger, as you pass by;
> As you are now, so was I;
> As I am, so you will be;
> So be prepared to follow me.

Years later someone wrote the following underneath this inscription:

> To follow you, I am not content;
> Till I know which way you went--

The Resurrection

The Resurrection is when our soul/spirit reunites with our body. The intermediate state then comes to an end and our final reward or punishment awaits us, depending on our relationship with the Lord Jesus Christ. The Bible is very clear that everyone will be raised from the dead, but that there will be two very different outcomes for the resurrected: one will be

---

[4]Thiessen, ibid, page 340.

to eternal life and the other to eternal condemnation.

1. The Old Testament predicts it:

- <u>Job 19:26</u> *And though after my skin worms destroy this body, yet in my flesh shall I see God.*

- <u>Psalm 16:10</u> *For thou wilt not leave my soul to Sheol; neither wilt thou suffer thy holy one to see corruption.*

- <u>Psalm 49:15</u> *But God will redeem my soul from the power of the grave: for he shall receive me.*

- <u>Psalm 71:20</u> *...and shalt bring me up again from the depths of the earth.*

- <u>Hosea 13:14</u> *"I will ransom them from the power of the grave; I will redeem them from death: O death, I will be thy plagues; O grave, I will be thy destruction: repentance shall be hid from mine eyes.*

- <u>Daniel 12:2:</u> *And many of them that sleep in the dust of the earth shall awake, some to everlasting life, and some to shame and everlasting contempt.*

2. Christ Confirms Affirms it:

- <u>John 5:28-29</u> *"Do not marvel at this; for the hour is coming in which all who are in the graves will hear His voice29 "and come forth—those who have done good, to the resurrection of life, and those who have done evil, to the resurrection of condemnation."*

- John 6:40 ...*and I will raise him up at the last day.*

- John 11:25: *Jesus said unto her I am the resurrection, and the life: he that believeth in me, though he were dead, yet shall he live.*

3. Paul Speaks of it:

- Acts 24:15 *And have hope toward God, which they themselves also allow, that there shall be a resurrection of the dead, both of the just and unjust.*

- I Corinthians 15:22-26 *For as in Adam all die, even so in Christ shall all be made alive. 23 But every man in his own order: Christ the first fruits; afterward they that are Christ's at his coming. 24 Then cometh the end, when he shall have delivered up the kingdom to God, even the Father; when he shall have put down all rule and all authority and power. 25 For he must reign, till he hath put all enemies under his feet. 26 The last enemy that shall be destroyed is death.*

- I Corinthians 15:51-52 *Behold, I show you a mystery; We shall not all sleep, but we shall all be changed, 52 In a moment, in the twinkling of an eye, at the last trump: for the trumpet shall sound, and the dead shall be raised incorruptible, and we shall be changed.*

- II Corinthians 4:14: *Knowing that he, which raised up the Lord Jesus shall raise up us also by Jesus, and shall present us with you.*

- I Thessalonians 4:16 *For the Lord himself shall descend from heaven with a shout, with the voice of the archangel, and with the trump of God: and the dead in Christ shall rise first.*

4. Revelation Fulfils It:

- Revelation 20:4 *And I saw thrones, and they sat upon them, and judgement was given unto them: and I saw the souls of them that were beheaded for the witness of Jesus, and for the word of God, and which had not worshipped the beast, neither his image, neither had received his mark upon their foreheads, or in on their hands; and they lived and reigned with Christ a thousand years.*

The most important award in life is not the Nobel Peace Prize, Order of Australia, or an Olympic Gold Medal: it is to be part of the first resurrection. Your relationship with the Lord Jesus Christ will determine which resurrection you will be. Make sure it is the right one.

For the righteous, eternity beckons.

REVIEW QUESTIONS:

1. What is the definition of the intermediate state?
2. What happens to the righteous in the intermediate state?
3. What happens to the unrighteous?
4. At the coming of Jesus Christ, what happens to the righteous?
5. At the Great White Throne Judgement, what happens to the unrighteous?[i]

---

2 Maccabees 12:42-45

42 Betook themselves unto prayer, and besought him that the sin committed might wholly be put out of remembrance. Besides, that noble Judas exhorted the people to keep themselves from sin, forsomuch as they saw before their eyes the things that came to pass for the sins of those that were slain.43 And when he had made a gathering throughout the company to the sum of two thousand drachms of silver, he sent it to Jerusalem to offer a sin offering, doing therein very well and honestly, in that he was mindful of the resurrection:44 For if he had not hoped that they that were slain should have risen again, it had been superfluous and vain to pray for the dead.45 And also in that he perceived that there was great favour laid up for those that died godly, it was an holy and good thought. Whereupon he made a reconciliation for the dead, that they might be delivered from sin.

[ii]The following passages are offered regarding the doctrine of the resurrection

Part Six

Eschatology from the Book of Revelation

Part six

Chapter Twelve

Take Another Look At Revelation

It was the subject of some of history's all-time bestsellers. Even with the transition to the third millennium A.D. complete, the future will be pondered afresh. This interest in the world tomorrow is something the church would do well to cultivate and address.

For students of the Bible who are prepared to speak to the world about things to come, the question is:

What would you say about the Book of Revelation?

Revelation: The Snorkeler's View

Even as a teacher of Eschatology, this author had the following comments about this important book:

> Revelation is full of mysteries and symbolism. Seven churches receive personalized letters from Jesus, but He rebukes most of them in very strong terms. One church, called Ephesus, is doing all the right actions but He still threatens to remove their candlestick. Another called Laodicea is so lukewarm that He threatens to spew them out of His mouth. More disturbing—enough so to scare you out of your wits-- is the array of cataclysmic activities this book describes. Seven seals, seven trumpets, and seven bowl judgements are poured out on an impenitent earth, all increasing in ferocity as time goes on. We learn

about devils, antichrists, false prophets and the mark of the beast, the most concentrated form of evil imaginable. An alarming amount of martyrdom ensues, instigated by the hideous whore of Babylon. This dangerous woman is Herodias, Delilah and Jezebel all wrapped into one and amplified one-thousand fold. She becomes intoxicated on the blood of the saints. Add to this the massive death toll of unbelievers and you have a depressing description that is breathlessly traumatic. By the time we get to the good news...where Christ returns, defeats the devil, vanquishes His foes, sets up His kingdom, and leads us into eternity, we are so devastated and exhausted; we can scarcely enjoy the glories of the New Jerusalem.

Is this how God wants us to understand the last book of the Bible?

It is basically the snorkeler's view of Revelation: dog paddling through the water near the surface. While you get some aquatic experience, it is exceedingly shallow. A better approach is to scuba dive, where you go down deep and see things that leave the other behind. That is why a good, in-depth Bible study, particularly the previously mentioned inductive one, will help bring a clear, mature, and exceedingly accurate interpretation.

This author did precisely that, inductively studying Revelation over a period of several months. From this wonderful experience emerged six outline points of what this book is really about, so foundational that scholars from all different eschatological persuasions should have no problem agreeing on these. Hence, this chapter is entitled take another look at Revelation.

Point One: Revelation is About Jesus Christ

The Revelation of Jesus Christ, which God gave Him to show His servants; things which must shortly take place—Revelation 1:1

As noted above, the view from the snorkel mask is a book about mysteries, symbols, and flamboyant evil. But nothing could be further from the truth. While the title of the book in the Greek text is apokalypsis Ioannou, meaning the "Revelation of John," this first verse gives the correct title, namely *apokalypsis Iesou Christou*, or "The Revelation of Jesus Christ."

The very first thing that the reader will discover is that this "revelation" is not about devils or antichrists...it is specifically and exclusively about Jesus Christ (by the way, avoid calling the book "Revelations" because it is not many revelations but one...Jesus' Revelation).

This revelation is not just the humble itinerant preacher of the Gospels, walking by the Sea of Galilee. It is also the glorified Son of God reigning from His heavenly throne, clearly and authoritatively speaking to His Church about the things that will quickly take place. He is mentioned explicitly, directly and gloriously in seventeen out of twenty-two chapters.

Since the Bible is "christo-centric," we believe that every one of the sixty-six books of the Bible has a portrait of Christ. This concept was both popularized and immortalized in Oral Robert's 1954 sermon, *The Fourth Man*, where he asks rhetorically and with great anointing, "Who is this fourth man in the Nebuchadnezzar's fiery furnace?" Then the evangelist proceeds to give the portraits of Christ found in the books of the Bible: He is the seed of the woman in Genesis; He is the burning bush in Exodus, etc.

> *...Revelation is not about devils and antichrists ... it is specifically and exclusively about Jesus Christ...*

Yet no other book of the Bible, including the four gospels, gives more vibrant descriptions and majestic titles for Jesus than Revelation. Here is a sample:

- *the faithful witness;*
- *the first begotten of the dead;*
- *the prince of the kings of the earth;*
- *Unto him that loved us;*
- *washed us from our sins in his own blood (1:5);*
- *Alpha and Omega;*
- *the beginning and the ending;*
- *which is, and which was, and which is to come;*
- *the Almighty (1:8);*
- *the first and the last (1:11);*
- *I am he that liveth, and was dead;*
- *behold, I am alive for evermore;*
- *Amen; and have the keys of hell and of death (1:18);*
- *he that holdeth the seven stars in his right hand;*
- *who walketh in the midst of the seven golden candlesticks (2:1);*
- *was dead, and is alive (2:8);*
- *Son of God, who hath his eyes like unto a flame of fire, and his feet are like fine brass (2:18);*
- *he that is holy;*
- *he that is true;*
- *he that hath the key of David;*

- *he that openeth, and no man shutteth; and shutteth, and no man openeth (3:7);*
- *These things saith the Amen;*
- *the faithful and true witness;*
- *the beginning of the creation of God (3:14);*
- *behold, the Lion of the tribe of Judah;*
- *the Root of David;*
- *hath prevailed to open the book, and to loose the seven seals thereof (5:5);*
- *Faithful and True;*
- *in righteousness he doth judge and make war (9:11);*
- *His name is called The Word of God (9:13);*
- *KING OF KINGS, AND LORD OF LORDS (19:16);*
- *I am the root and the offspring of David;*
- *And the bright and morning star (22:16).—Authorized King James Version.*

This is not a comprehensive list, but sufficient enough to build and sustain the case that Revelation is about Jesus Christ. You learn about Him present tense, future, and forever.

Point Two: Revelation is About God

Again, we argue that the forces of evil are minor players in the great stage of Revelation. The book is divine and so is its subject. In short, Revelation is about God.

In chapter four you are given a guided tour into a place that is beyond the realm of this world. It is called the Throne of God. The inspired words of this chapter on their own still cannot convey the full splendor and majesty of this center of the universe. Apparently, what the twenty-four elders saw in the throne room was so breathtaking and awesome that they felt compelled to collapse—in unison—from their thrones and cast their crowns before Almighty God at His throne. They say in one accord:

You are worthy, O Lord, to receive glory and honor and power; for you created all things, and by your will they exist and were created.—Revelation 4:11

Only the "Revelation of Jesus Christ," the spotless, sinless, majestic, overcoming, resurrected Lamb of God, could possibly afford us this view of the holiest precincts of all.

But there is more. On doing a count of the references to God and goodness, versus the devil and evil, we come across some interesting statistics:

References to Good and Evil in Revelation	
Good	Evil
"Jesus" is mentioned 12 times	"Satan" is mentioned 7 times
"Lamb" is mentioned 24 times	"Serpent" is mentioned 4 times
"Lord" is mentioned 25 times	"Dragon" is mentioned 12 times
"Almighty" is mentioned 8 times	"The Beast" is mentioned 25 times
"Spirit" is mentioned 16 times	"Harlot" is mentioned 4 times
"Blessed" is mentioned 7 times	"Babylon" is mentioned 6 times
"God" is mentioned 90 times	
"Jerusalem" is mentioned 3 times	
"Christ" is mentioned 4 times[1]	
Total:	Total:
189 References	58 References

[1] The actual Name "Christ" is mentioned ten times in Revelation but in six instances it is part of the name "Jesus Christ," which is mentioned six times. Since the name "Jesus" is mentioned 12 times, and in order to avoid duplication, the name "Christ" is mentioned only four times on its own in Revelation.

When you add up the references, it is 189 times in God's column versus 58 times for the devil and evil, over three to one. This is nothing short of a landslide for God! Thus, we can confidently affirm that Revelation is a Book about God.

Point Three: Revelation is About Blessing

Without question all Scripture is inspired by God and all is profitable (II Timothy 3:16), which means that those who hear and do what it says will be prosperous, fruitful, effective, joyful, and blessed. Scripture also pronounces curses on those who are disobedient (Deuteronomy 28:15). But only in the book of Revelation is there a written promise of blessing for those who "read and heed" what it says. This promise is found near the very beginning:

> *Blessed is he who reads and those who hear the words of this prophecy, and keep those things which are written in it; for the time is near*— Revelation 1:3

This is an important point, because if one takes the snorkeler's point-of-view, it would appear that Revelation is a confusing, terrifying portrait of the future. Yet God's purpose in Revelation is to "reveal" His Son Jesus Christ as He is present tense and forever. The second purpose is to bless all those who listen and obey what He says. Such people are truly building their houses on a rock (Matthew 7:25).

God takes the blessings of Revelation so seriously that He installs a strong warning in the very last chapter of the book: if anyone adds to the words of the prophecy of this book, God will add to him the plagues that are written (22:18) **and** if anyone takes away from the words of the book of this prophecy, God shall subtract from them their part from the Book of Life, the holy city, and the things that are written in this book (22:19). Why such severity? Because God does not want to dilute the integrity of the blessings He has prepared for His redeemed.

Something wonderful must be in store for us from this Book of Revelation when it comes with a guaranteed promise to bless from Almighty God Himself!

Point Four: Revelation is About Justice

So far, Revelation has been presented in a very positive light. It is a book about Jesus Christ, God, and blessing. But what about those terrifying judgements: seven seals, seven trumpets, and seven bowls? As individual judgements, they are frightful—war, antichrist, martyrdom, one-third of the vegetation destroyed, one-third of humanity killed—but put together they are truly apocalyptic. Why, on earth, does a loving, wonderful God allow such catastrophes to hit the earth?

In order for this world to function correctly, we need justice. Justice is defined as "the administration of law; the act of determining rights and assigning rewards or punishments."[2] The very character of God, including His holiness and righteousness, can only be maintained if He rewards righteousness and punishes wickedness. But because all people possess a lack of righteousness, and could never rectify this situation in their own strength, God demonstrated His love for us that while we were yet sinners Christ died for us. Christ's atoning work on the Cross fulfills God's twin character qualities: justice and mercy.

---

[2] http://www.onelook.com/?w=justice&ls=a Accessed 16 March 2006.

Anyone who is even a casual observer of the world scene knows that the world lacks justice. High-profile individuals either avoid their day in court or, if indicted, are released due to highly paid cunning lawyers. Innocent people, however, can suffer grievously through no fault of their own.

Jesus promises that God will avenge the injustices of His elect—speedily (Luke 18:7-8) and James 5:9 says that the Judge is standing at the door. Justice is coming, but how?

In Revelation, we see the righteous justice of God, either as judgement to a vile, evil, sin-riddled, impenitent world or rewards for those who lived for God during their time on earth. Yes, the Judge of the whole earth shall do right! (Genesis 18:25).

At first glance, it would appear that these destructive events are the devil's work. But this is clearly not the case. These cataclysms are not devil-inspired chicanery but God's righteous judgement. Remember, when it comes to the judgements of Revelation, it is not Satan who is running riot throughout world. It is God who controls these traumatic events in faithfulness to His character and elect.

For example, what kick starts the judgements is the breaking of the seven seals. But who does this? It is not Satan. He is not worthy. In fact, the only one who is worthy is Jesus Christ (5:5), and it is He who will break the seals that send the four horsemen of the apocalypse riding into the field (6:1-8). It is the angels of God who sound the seven trumpet judgements (8:6) and likewise seven angels—not the devil or demons—who are commanded to "*Go, pour out the seven bowls of God's wrath on the earth*" (16:1).

God is definitely in charge during this time and He is pouring out His long delayed wrath on a hardened, rebellious, and evil world. The needful culmination of this period is the much-deserved destruction of Babylon (18:10), the beast, false prophet, and eventually Satan himself (20:10). Sin, Satan, death, and evil, will finally be overcome and overthrown! This is the justice of God and for every true believer we can take comfort in this. More than that, we can rejoice.

Point Five: Revelation is About the Church

While the original recipients of many Bible books was Israel, or a specific group of people, Revelation is truly a book that is addressed to the Church, the Body of Christ, consisting of all born-again believers, both Jew & Gentile, throughout the church age. The Church is called to receive several things, including: His testimony (1:1-2); blessing for hearing and obeying (1:3); God's grace and peace (1:4); love of Christ who washes us from our sins in His own blood (1:5); the label of "kings and priests" to God (1:6). Many more benefits flow on from these.

In addition to being addressed to the universal church, it also targets seven local congregations found in Asia Minor, now known as modern Turkey. Their individual letters are found in chapters two and three. Each letter has a commendation, criticism, task to fulfill, and a promise to the overcomer.

While the message of these two chapters is to real congregations of the first century, the principles and warning espoused apply to the church throughout the ages. Special mention should be made of the warnings to Ephesus, the first church, and Laodicea, the seventh and last church.

Ephesus received the magnificent epistle called "Ephesians." This literary treasure to the Church shows us who we are "in Christ." We receive a new and permanent identity, a lofty celestial position, and a priceless inheritance. There are no rebukes in this epistle, mostly blessings but also a solemn warning to put on the "whole armor of God" (6:10). Chapter 2 Verse 6 says *"and raised us up together, and made us sit together in the heavenly places in Christ."* How can one feel low when they are seated above? So Ephesus, as a young and dynamic church, was doing well in Paul's day. They clearly had a heavenly perspective.

But by the time of Revelation things had changed. Ephesus had become an established church, which was still properly functioning and doing the right things. However, Jesus now had something against them: they had left their first love (2:4). This was no misdemeanor. So serious was their departure from the "first love" and "first works" that Jesus threatens to remove their lamp stand from its place (2:5).

How could a church, which had an earlier message of identity, position, and blessing, now be threatened with its removal from its place? Verse 5 of chapter two says *"Remember therefore from where you have fallen."* In Ephesians, the church was seated in the heavenly places. By Revelation, they had fallen from the heavenly places without even knowing it. They were middle-aged, routine, and simply going through the motions.

What was the solution? Repent and do the first works (2:5). Repentance, which means to change your mind, attitude, and actions, is the only way to get off the ground and to be catapulted into the heavenly places again. This indispensable but much neglected Bible word is not just for sinners who want to come to Christ, but it is also for Christians who have gotten off the track.

How often are we to repent? Seventy times seven! As often as we fail to faithfully follow Jesus. Chances are that if an individual is not practicing the principles of God's Word, walking in the Spirit, or living a life of obedience to the Lord, he or she will need to repent. Joy Dawson says that repentance means "sorry enough to quit!" Without repentance, we risk having our candlestick removed from its place.

Let us look at the other church, which has its own set of unique challenges. The Church at Laodicea is described by Christ as neither cold nor hot. He wishes they were either one or the other. At least if they are cold, their position would be clear to all. But as it is, the Laodicean church is neither fully Christian nor fully heathen, not fit for hell nor ready for heaven, avoiding nominalism but far from revival.

What is so frightening is that the Laodicean attitude is so prevalent in the western church today. This mindset says I am rich, have become wealthy, and have need of nothing (3:17). Yet from Christ's point-of-view they are wretched, miserable, poor, blind, and naked. It is their materialism and apathy that had cooled down any fire they once had for the Lord. Because of their state of lukewarmness Christ threatens to do more than merely remove a candlestick from its place. He promises to spew out of His mouth (3:16).

In these postmodern therapeutic days, where the goal is to help people "feel good" rather than become good, some would say that Jesus must have hated this church so much because He spoke to them in this manner. On the contrary, Jesus is actually so brim full of love for this congregation that He cannot speak any other way. He says in Verse 19 of Chapter 3, *"As many as I love, I rebuke and chasten. Therefore be zealous and repent."* To be zealous or *Zeleuo* is to spark the fire again, so that lukewarmness will be converted to boiling hot.

Note that the word "repent" is used again for the church. Laodicea is heading in the wrong direction. If it would "repent," turn around, and go the way of zeleuo, then they will inherit the best gift of all. It is time that we recapture this wonderful word of repentance, for until we do, revival will continue to tarry in the Laodicean churches of today.

Note Jesus invitation in verse 20. He stands at the door and knocks. If you will open the door and let Him in, He will come in and dine with you. This passage has been used liberally in evangelistic meetings to invite the unbeliever to come to faith in Christ. While this author has no objection of the use of Revelation 3:20 in evangelism, please remember that the original context of this verse was not to the unbeliever, but to the Church.

When you ponder this, it is incredible: Jesus Christ is head of the Church, which He purchased with His own shed blood. He is the legal owner and occupier. And yet here He is, graciously and patiently waiting outside the door of His own church, asking if He could come in. This is positively absurd—and yet is very real. Laodicean churches, you have a choice: let Christ come back into His church or risk being spewed from His mouth.

---

[3]*2206.* zhlovw ze μ lo á o μ, dzay-lo á -o or zhleuvw ze μ le á uo μ dzay-loo-o; from 2205; to have warmth of feeling for or against:— affect, covet (earnestly), (have) desire, (move with) envy, be jealous over, (be) zealous (-ly affect). From James Strong, *New Strong's dictionary of Hebrew and Greek words [computer file], electronic ed., Logos Library System,* (Nashville: Thomas Nelson) 1997, c1996.

However, if Laodicean churches are zealous, repent, and overcome, they get the greatest prize of all—they can sit with Christ on His throne (3:21). No other church was given this opportunity, even though they were more righteous. This is simply another example of the amazing grace of God. Churches worldwide would do well to take heed to the warnings given to Ephesus and Laodicea, for if they repent, the rewards will be nothing short of awesome.

Point Six: Revelation is About Eternity

While the Bible outlines God's plan for mankind—namely establishing His eternal kingdom and blessing all those who cooperate with Him—very little is said in Scripture about eternity. This is all the more remarkable when you consider that the bulk of our time will be spent (99.99999999999%) in this little spoken-about period. Out of 1,189 chapters in Scripture, less than two are devoted to the subject of eternity. They happen to be the last two chapters of the Bible, Revelation 21 and 22.

Revelation gives us a glimpse of eternity—obviously, with only limited detail, but sufficient enough to help us taste of the glory of the age to come. Contrast the picture of Revelation 21-22, to that at the end of chapter 20, when the ungodly are cast into the lake of fire, and your worship of God should become whole hearted and spontaneous. Eternity is not long enough to thank Jesus Christ for saving us from such a horrendous destination.

Revelation is about eternity, but more will be said in the final chapter regarding the "Eternal State."

REVIEW QUESTIONS:

1. What are the six main points about the Book of Revelation?
2. Revelation Chapter Four gives us the view of something not found in the same detail anywhere else in Scripture. What is it?
3. How many references to God and godly things are found in this book? And to evil?
4. Why is the justice of God, as displayed by the seal, trumpet, and bowl judgements, good news for the believer?
5. How much information in Scripture is given on the topic of "eternity?"

Chapter Thirteen

Chronology of Pre-Tribulation Events

Pre-Tribulation Events

World Wars, global governance, Israel and the Middle East, a Jewish Jerusalem—these are some of the topics we can expect in the times leading up to the end. Our approach to these end-time prophecies will be literal and chronological. When it comes to the pre-tribulation events, there is no time-frame of when they will happen, or how much time gap there will be between these events and the tribulation. Our purpose is to highlight some of these events and inspire you to become a more diligent student of Scripture.

We have looked at the topic of Personal or Individual or Invisible Eschatology. Now, we will look at "International Eschatology." The Day of the Lord is a term that will be used frequently. For our purposes, the Day of the Lord includes the tribulation period, which are the birthpangs of the coming kingdom, as well as the thousand year kingdom period itself, known as the Millennium.

Time of Deception

The very first exhortation Christ gives is to *"Take heed that no one deceives you"* (Matthew 24:4). Of itself, deception is nothing new and has been around since the Garden of Eden. But the nature of this deception will be larger, more official, and with a feigned legitimacy by invoking the name of Christ. Many false Christs will come and deceive many (v. 5). With so many roads and voices out there, it is important to keep your eyes on the real Jesus—the Light of the world (John 8:12), because whoever follows Him will never be in darkness.

In order to follow the real Jesus, we need to be students of the Word and filled with the Spirit. God's Word is a lamp to our feet and a light to our path (Psalm 119: 105). Considering the on-going Biblical illiteracy found in Christendom today, such deception becomes all the more plausible.

International Turmoil

In the Olivet Discourse Jesus speaks about *"wars and rumors of wars," "nation will rise against nation, and kingdom against kingdom,"* accompanied by famines, pestilences, and earthquakes in many places. Fruchtenbaum shares some exciting background to the earlier phrases. The Bereshit Rabbah says:

> If you shall see kingdoms rising against each other in turn, then give heed and note the footsteps of the Messiah.

He also quotes the Zohar Chadash, which says:

> At the time wars shall be stirred up in the world. Nation shall be against nation and city against city; much distress shall be renewed against the enemy of the Israelites. [1]

---

[1] Arnold Fruchtenbaum, *The Footsteps of the Messiah*, Tustin CA: Ariel Press, 1990, page 64.

While history has been replete with wars, only in the twentieth century has the phenomenon of a world war coming into being. Not only were empires colliding and collapsing during the First World War, but also diverse nations from different points of the globe came together to fight one another. When one considers that in 1915 troops from as far away as South Africa, Canada, India, Australia, and New Zealand, fought at the rocky outcropping called Gallipolli in Turkey on behalf of "king and country" does one appreciate how unique and devastating a world war can be. Casualties of both world wars are in the tens of millions.

But massive death tolls would not just come due to war. Famines, earthquakes, and pestilence would add dramatically to the final number. While there is some debate as to whether the amount of earthquakes has increased in the last century, there is no question that earthquakes are becoming more deadly, with mortality rates in the tens and hundreds of thousands. Famines have caused millions to die in the last century and pestilences can also be a grim reaper. The 1918 Spanish flu pandemic claimed millions of lives. If the Avian bird flu ever turns against humans en mass, we face even higher numbers.

Israel and the Middle East

When it comes to the modern day nation of Israel, rarely can anyone be neutral. It stirs up debate and passion like no other nation. But it is not just in the geo-political sphere that this takes place—it is also in the theological realm, too. Among the monotheists, only Islam seems to be unified when it comes to its opinion of Israel. Jews are not necessarily in total agreement, because some ultra-orthodox Jews believe that only the Messiah can re-establish Israel. Thus they view the modern state of Israel as a human counterfeit, founded by socialists and agnostic European Ashkenazi Jews.

Christian theologians are even more divided, with some stating flatly that God is finished with the "Christ-rejecting" Jews while others contend that the unconditional theocratic covenantal promises hold true for Israel, no matter what. Some amillennialists were caught off-guard with Israel's rebirth in 1948. But even among the more literalistic premillennialists some feel that the modern state of Israel could not possibly be a fulfilment of prophecy since the Jews have returned to Palestine in a state of unbelief regarding the person of Jesus, and that many of them are not even religious Jews.

In assessing the prophetic importance of modern Israel, or otherwise, it is crucial that we look beyond headlines, propaganda, and some of the painful issues afflicting the Jews and Arabs. The Palestinian Arab history since 1948 has been particularly tragic and exceedingly difficult to solve, but to what extent their suffering is caused by Israel and/or by their own leaders, is subject to debate. We must reject any notion that tries to make this tragic conflict "black and white," as if one side is completely good and the other utterly evil. Both sides have suffered grievously (and not always at the hands of the other), the involvement of other parties complicates the situation, and apart from a divine solution, only statecraft of the highest order will help manage, if not solve, this intractable state of affairs. The outside world would do well to pray, practice compassion, and seek understanding and God's justice of the issues at hand.

The Apostle Paul speaks about "the mystery of Israel" (Romans 11:25),[2] and God's dealings with Israel constitute one of the great mysteries of

Scripture. But unlike worldly mysteries, God's mystery is revealed to His people.

People who practice more literal interpretation of prophetic passages will invariably conclude that God has an end-time purpose for the Jewish people; others say that due to Jewish unbelief, God has replaced them with the Church. In any case, passages used to sustain the claim that the Jews/Israel will be gathered into Palestine in the last days include: Isaiah 11:11-12; Jeremiah 16: 14-15; 23:7-8; Ezekiel 20:33-38; 22:17-22; Amos 9:14-15.

The passage from Isaiah 11 is particularly interesting:

11 It shall come to pass in that day that the LORD shall set His hand again the second time to recover the remnant of His people who are left, from Assyria and Egypt, from Pathros and Cush, from Elam and Shinar, from Hamath and the islands of the sea. 12 He will set up a banner for the nations, and will assemble the outcasts of Israel, and gather together the dispersed of Judah from the four corners of the earth.

These verses say that God will regather Israel "the second time," which appears to be just before the millennial kingdom. So when was the first time? The return from Babylon was prophesied, and fulfilled, but it did not encompass the international breadth to which Isaiah refers.

---

[2] "Mystery" speaks of God's once concealed, now revealed, plan of salvation through Jesus Christ. The Gospel is a "mystery which was kept secret since the world began" (Rom. 16:25). This mystery was made known by God through prophecy to the Apostle Paul and the Church (1 Cor. 2:7; Eph. 6:19; Col. 4:3). "Mystery" also refers to the future resurrection of true believers (1 Cor. 15:51), the culmination of all things in Christ (Eph. 1:9), the inclusion of Gentiles with Israel in the church (Eph. 3:3–9), the salvation of "all Israel" in the future (Rom. 11:25), of marriage and Christ's union with the Church (Ephesians 5:30-32), lawlessness during the tribulation period (2 Thess. 2:7), and the godliness of Christ (1 Tim. 3:16).

Could it be that the first international regathering occurs before the tribulation period? Zephaniah 1:14-18 speaks about the Day of the Lord and preceding this Day is 2:1-2, where Israel is told to *"gather yourselves together...O undesirable (shameless) nation."* So the first international regathering will happen both pre-faith and pre-tribulation, while the second happens pre-millennial and in faith.

Jerusalem

While technically a separate issue, Jerusalem looms large on the international agenda of world hot spots. "The Jerusalem Question" has vexed diplomats for most of the twentieth century. Prior to 1917, the Ottoman Empire was the last internationally recognized undisputed owner/ruler of the Holy City. Since the British succeeded the Ottomans after the First World War, the issue of who would own and rule Jerusalem has only increased in acrimony and fury.

In 1947, the United Nations voted to partition Palestine into a Jewish and Arab state, with the City of Jerusalem become a corpus separatum, meaning that it would belong neither to Palestine or Israel, but to the international community. The UN would administer the city. The first Arab-Israeli War in 1948 resulted in the city's partition between Israel and Jordan, with neither side inclined to hand over their portion to the UN. Then in 1967, Israel captured the Jordanian sector, re-united the city, and annexed the whole as its eternal, indivisible capital. The phrase: *"Jerusalem is not negotiable"* became common currency afterwards.

Is the 1967 Jewish takeover of Jerusalem after 1,900 years a fulfilment of prophecy? This question is invariably linked to that of Israel: if the modern regathering of the Jews to Palestine and the re-birth of Israel is a fulfilment of prophecy, then so, too, is the Jewish conquest and acquisition of Jerusalem. You cannot have one without the other.

With few exceptions, the world community does not recognize Israel's sovereignty over Jerusalem. Most foreign embassies are in Tel Aviv, sixty-five kilometres away.

One key end-time passage is Zechariah 12:1-3, where "Judah" and "Jerusalem" become the centre of international controversy and conflict. In fact, there will be a siege of Jerusalem, which will become the heavy stone whereby the nations of the earth will be cut in pieces. In chapter 14:1-4, the Day of the Lord will have an international invasion of Jerusalem, followed by the second coming of Christ.

Again, it would appear that at a literal glance Judah and Jerusalem will have Jews living it before the second coming of Christ. Not only that, but in another section, we looked at the prospects of an end-time Jewish temple (see Daniel 9:27; Matthew 24:15; II Thessalonians 2:3-4; and Revelation 11:1-2). This would imply that the Jews control the Temple Mount and, by extension, the city of Jerusalem. Today, Israel has Jerusalem, and holds the keys to the Temple Mount, but it is owned and administered by the Muslim Waqf as an Islamic holy site.

---

[3] In 1980, the government of Israeli Prime Minister Menachem Begin reaffirmed Israeli sovereignty over Jerusalem, as the eternal and indivisible capital of Israel, through the passage of the "Basic Law," which is a building block of Israel's de facto constitution. After passage of this law, some of the few remaining foreign embassies in Jerusalem moved to Tel Aviv, where most of the foreign diplomatic community resides. This reaction triggered the founding of what became the International Christian Embassy of Jerusalem (ICEJ), which convened its annual Feast of Tabernacles celebration from that year until now.

In the natural, the prospects for a future Jewish temple are very low, not only because of Islamic and international opposition, but also Jewish secularized indifference to such a religious building. But a hundred years ago, the prospects of a reconstituted Jewish state in Palestine looked very bleak as well. In the Middle East, expect the unexpected.

Gog & Magog

Some scholars consider this an important pre-tribulation event. The reason is that almost all, if not all, of the key ingredients for fulfilment are available today for the first time in history. Prudence would dictate the need to "watch and pray." While there are also the options of this prophecy being fulfilled sometime during the Tribulation, including the Campaign of Armageddon, there is also a reference to Gog and Magog after the Millennium in Revelation 20. We need to keep an open mind on this subject and avoid dogmatism. See Chapter Nine for more information.

Global Governance

It may surprise many readers that the concept of "nation state" is relatively recent, to which the United States of America (1776) is one of the oldest. Prior to that, the world was run by empires of which many came out of Europe: Spain, Portugal, England, Germany, France, Austro-Hungary, Turkey (Ottoman), and Russia. The Chinese and Mongols also were imperial masters. Some of the above empires declined and fell before the First World War, while others collapsed after the war. Many colonies received their independence and became sovereign nations. Yet even while this was happening, the seedbed of global governance had been planted. After World War I, the League of Nations came into being, but after its demise the United Nations (1945) took its place.

Birthed right after the devastation of the Second World War, the UN's initial goal was to promote and foster world peace and prevent any future world wars. Yet the world body has grown both in bureaucracy and influence, passing all kinds of regulations, calling them "international law," and expecting member states to abide by these things. This notion alone can undermine national sovereignty and democracy, especially since those who make the rules are unelected, unaccountable, and unconnected by those who are expected to keep them. As Europe heads towards becoming a superstate and other regions of the world look to uniting into regional blocs, the components for global governance, known also as a one-world government, are ready to be assembled.

The key verses for this are Daniel 7:23-24:

23 "Thus he said: 'The fourth beast shall be a fourth kingdom on earth, which shall be different from all other kingdoms, and shall devour the whole earth, trample it and break it in pieces. 24 The ten horns are ten kings who shall arise from this kingdom. And another shall rise after them; he shall be different from the first ones, and shall subdue three kings.

This "fourth kingdom" which devours, tramples, and breaks in pieces the whole world, is the legs of iron, feet of iron and clay "imperial kingdom" found in Nebuchadnezzar's statue. It represents the one-world government.

From this fourth kingdom will emerge ten kingdoms. What or who these exactly will be is not yet clear, but it seems reasonable to assume that the ten kingdoms cover the entire world, and not just Europe and the West.

After the ten kingdoms emerge, the passage reads that "another shall rise after them," different from the first ones, and shall subdue three kings. This person is none other than the antichrist, who will be revealed before the tribulation period. A great falling away or apostasy will also happen and then antichrist comes to the stage, known as "the man of sin" and "son of perdition" (II Thessalonians 2:3).

So antichrist will be revealed before the Day of the Lord. During the period of the ten kingdoms while antichrist comes on the stage, there will be a period of "peace and safety," as recorded in I Thessalonians 5:1-3:

> *But concerning the times and the seasons, brethren, you have no need that I should write to you.2 For you yourselves know perfectly that the day of the Lord so comes as a thief in the night.3 For when they say, "Peace and safety!" then sudden destruction comes upon them, as labor pains upon a pregnant woman. And they shall not escape.*

The actual event which that will commence the tribulation is not the rapture of the Church. It is the fulfillment of Daniel 9:27f, which says "Then he shall confirm a covenant with many for one week...." Since this is the prophecy of Daniel's Seventy Weeks, which pertains to Israel, it is with Israel that the covenant is made and the "he" is the "prince that is to come" of verse 26, namely antichrist. So when such an agreement has been made between a charismatic, peace-making world ruler and Israel, then the countdown to Armageddon has begun.

As we see some exciting developments on the international front, we need to be prayerful, observant, non-dogmatic, gracious, charitable, and watchful. Again we hearken to the example of the Bereans, who searched the Scriptures daily to see if these things are so (Acts 17:11).

REVIEW QUESTIONS:

1. List the six headers in pre-tribulation events.
2. Which events do you see happening before your eyes?
3. Why are Israel and Jerusalem important end-time issues?

Chapter Fourteen

Chronology of the Tribulation

The Great Tribulation in Scripture

Some think that the Great Tribulation is only in the "spiritualized" Book of Revelation, or sprinkled lightly in the New Testament. Scripture is holistic and the doctrine of the tribulation is widely mentioned in both testaments. The following are phrases to describe the tribulation:

- *"Tribulation" (Deuteronomy 4:30);*
- *"The Day of Israel's Calamity" (Deuteronomy 32:35, Obadiah 12–14);*
- *70th Week (Daniel 9:27);*
- *"Jehovah's Strange Work & Jehovah's Strange Act" (Isaiah 28:21);*
- *"The Indignation" (Isaiah 26:20; Daniel 11:36);*
- *"The Overflowing Scourge (Isaiah 28:15,18);*
- *"The Day of Vengeance" (Isaiah 34:8, 35:4, 61:2);*
- *"The Year of Recompense" (Isaiah 34:8);*
- *"Time of Trouble" (Daniel 12:1; Zephaniah 1:15);*
- *"Time of Jacob's Trouble" (Jeremiah 30:7);*
- *"The Day of Wrath" (Zephaniah 1:15);*
- *"Day of Distress" (Zephaniah 1:15);*
- *"Day of Wasteness" (Zephaniah 1:15);*
- *"Day of Desolation" (Zephaniah 1:15);*
- *"Day of Darkness" (Zephaniah 1:15, Amos 5:18,20; Joel 2:2);*
- *"Day of Gloominess" (Zephaniah 1:15; Joel 2:2);*
- *"Day of Clouds" (Zephaniah 1:15; Joel 2:2);*

- *"Day of Thick Darkness" (Zephaniah 1:15; Joel 2:2);*
- *"Day of Trumpet" (Zephaniah 1:16);*
- *"Day of Alarm" (Zephaniah 1:16)*
- *"Day of the Lord" (I Thessalonians 5:2);*
- *"Wrath of God" (Revelation 15:1,7; 14:10,19:16:1);*
- *"Hour of Trial" (Revelation 3:10);*
- *"Great Day of the Wrath of the Lamb of God" (Revelation 6:16–17);*
- *"Wrath to Come" (I Thessalonians 1:10);*
- *"Wrath" (I Thessalonians 5:9; Revelation 11:18);*
- *"The Great Tribulation" (Matthew 24:21; Revelation 2:22; 7:14);*
- *"The Tribulation" (Matthew 24:29);*
- *"The Hour of Judgement"(Revelation 14:7).*

Why Does the Tribulation Happen?

The God of the Bible is described in wonderfully celestial terms as the One Who is all-powerful, all-present, all-knowing, all-loving, totally benevolent, and full of glory. Yet the tribulation period was forecasted millennia before the end-time. Why would such *a* wonderful God allow this horrible period of worldwide pain and destruction?

Recall the dream of Nebuchadnezzar where the great world empires are symbolized by a single statue made of several ingredients. This statue represents the "kingdoms of this world" and the "times of the Gentiles." The stone cut out of the mountain without hands hurls towards the statue, hitting it at the base, and causes its total destruction. We learned that the stone represents Christ and His kingdom, which abides forever. Apparently the statue does not disintegrate by itself; it is forced to its demised by the hurling stone.

When Revelation 11:15 says the kingdoms of this world have become the kingdoms of our Lord and of His Christ, there will be no smooth transition of power, like in a liberal democracy. It will be violent and forceful. Obviously, the worldly realms do not want to surrender their power and live under Messiah so they do what they can to resist. Such resistance will be futile, of course, but it does not stop them from trying.

The arrival of the coming messianic kingdom is likened to a woman in labour pains before the birth of her child. So preceding the joy of birth will be a season of pain. So the tribulation is the birth pangs of Christ's coming kingdom. It is mankind's rebellion.

Scripture teaches that the period known as the "Day of the Lord," which begins with the tribulation, is when God will destroy sinners and wickedness (Isaiah 13:9; Isaiah 24:19-20). He will also break the stubbornness of the chosen people (Daniel 12:5-7) so they will finally become compliant with His will; and once this happens, it will help institute a worldwide revival (Revelation 7:1-17) by Jewish evangelists. After all, if their unbelief caused the blessings of the Gospel to be spread to the whole Gentile world, then their brokenness and acceptance will mean life from the dead (Romans 11:15).

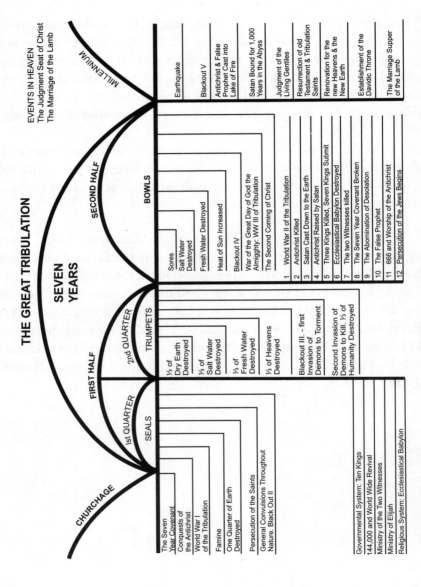

used with permission from: Dr. Arnold Fructenbaum, Ariel Ministries, www.ariel.org

The Great Tribulation: A Basic Outline

The seven-year tribulation period, known as Daniel's seventieth week, commences with the signing of the covenant between antichrist and Israel. The tribulation can be divided into two halves of three and a half years each, and the first half can be divided into two quarters. In the first quarter, you have the seven seal judgements; in the second quarter, the seven trumpet judgements; and in the second half are the seven bowl judgements. A series of events will also happen throughout the period of the first half of the tribulation, as well as in the middle.

I. <u>Tribulation Begins:</u> Signing of the Covenant between Israel and Antichrist (Daniel 9:27)

II. <u>First Half of the Tribulation</u> (3 1/2 Years)
    A. <u>First Quarter:</u> Seven Seal Judgements
    B. <u>Second Quarter:</u> Seven Trumpet Judgements
    C. <u>Throughout the First Half (first & second quarters):</u>
        1. The Ten Kingdoms
        2. The Rise of Ecclesiastical Babylon
        3. The 144,000 and worldwide evangelism
        4. The Ten Kings
        5. Ministry of the Two Witnesses

III. <u>Middle of the Tribulation</u>
    A. Covenant broken
    B. Satan cast down to earth
    C. Second great war
    D. Antichrist killed

E. Antichrist raised again by Satan

F. Two witnesses killed and rise again

G. Three kings subdued and seven submit

H. The rise of the false prophet

I. The abomination of desolation

J. 666 instituted and antichrist worshipped

K. Persecution of non-conformists begin

L. Ecclesiastical Babylon destroyed

IV. <u>Second Half of the Tribulation (3 1/2 Years)</u>

A. Seven Trumpet Judgements

B. Campaign from Armageddon, rather than Battle of Armageddon

C. Second Coming of Christ

The Seven Seal Judgements

Jesus Christ is the only one who has prevailed over everything and is worthy to open the scroll and break the seven seals. The breaking of these seals kick-starts the tribulation judgements. Remember all these judgements are God's way of punishing a vile, rebellious, and impenitent world system. The first four seals are also known as the "Four Horsemen of the Apocalypse."

Seal One: the White Horse and Antichrist (6:1-2)

This speaks of antichrist and his conquests. While the name "antichrist" is not used at all in Revelation, he is well described in other Bible books, including:

1. *"Seed of Satan" (Genesis 3:15);*
2. *"The little horn" (Daniel 7:8);*
3. *"King of fierce countenance" (Daniel 8:23);*
4. *"The prince that shall come" (Daniel 9:26);*
5. *"The desolator" (Daniel 9:27);*
6. *"The man of sin, son of perdition" (II Thessalonians 2:3);*
7. *"The lawless one" (II Thessalonians 2:8);*
8. *"The antichrist" (I John 2:22);*
9. *"The beast" (Revelation 11:7).*

There has been much speculation as to the identity of the antichrist. Many nominations have been given, including Roman popes, Adolph Hitler, Joseph Stalin, Mao Zedong, Saddam Hussein, and even former U.S. Secretary of State Henry Kissinger. One clue to his identification is Daniel 9:26, which speaks of the "people of the prince who is to come." Many commentators believe the "people" come from the Roman Empire, for they are the ones who destroyed the Jewish Temple after Daniel's day in A.D. 70. So it is assumed he would be a Roman (an identification which has satisfied many anti-papists).

However, remember that the better term is "imperial empire," which would broaden the antichrist catchments area from the city of Rome to the entire breadth of the Old Roman Empire, including southern Europe, the Middle East, and North Africa. Since the prototype of antichrist was the Gentile Seleucid Syrian ruler called Antiochus IV or "Epiphanes" of the second century B.C., and the period itself is called the "Times of the Gentiles," it seems more than reasonable that antichrist will be a Gentile. But would the Jews ever worship a Gentile? Well, they appeared to do so in Antiochus day, so is it really inconceivable that a secularlized, globalized Jewry would worship a Gentile in the in the future?

Character of Antichrist

It is important to go beyond the Book of Revelation to see what is written about this important yet diabolical character. Some key passages include Daniel 8:23-25; 11:36-39; Genesis 3:15; II Thessalonians 2:9. Points of interest include:

* He will be a king of fierce countenance (Daniel 8:23);
* His power will be mighty, but it will not be his power (Daniel 8:24);
* He was be destructive and temporarily prosperous (Daniel 8:24);
* He will be cunning and deceitful (Daniel 8:25);
* He will magnify himself in his heart (Daniel 8:25);
* He shall destroy many in their prosperity (Daniel 8:25);
* He will even try to rise up against the prince of princes, but he will be broken supernaturally (Daniel 8:25);
* He will do his own will (Daniel 11:36);
* He will exalt and magnify himself above every god, speaking blasphemy against the true God (Daniel 11:36);
* He shall prosper until (God's) wrath overtakes him (Daniel 11:36);
* He will magnify himself against God, gods, and even women (Daniel 11:37);
* He shall worship a new god, the god of fortresses-Satan-and will temporarily prosper and conquer accordingly (Daniel 11:38-39);
* He is the seed of Satan and will be judged accordingly (Genesis 3:15);
* He will do the work of Satan with power, signs, and lying wonders (II Thessalonians 2:9);

The coming and rise of antichrist is a portent of even worse things to come.

Seal Two: Red Horse and War (6:3-4)

The antichrist will sign a covenant with Israel but it will be a "covenant with death" (Isaiah 28:15, 18) and so war will be the major means of bringing death and destruction. There are three major wars during the tribulation: this one, one in the middle, and the final one at Armageddon.

Seal Three: Black Horse and Famine (6:5-6)

Famine can be the result of natural causes or war; in this case it is the latter. Food will be scarce because of this war, but the preservation of the oil and wine means there will be some means of healing wounds (Luke 10:34). So this act of mercy from God, as symbolized by the oil and wine, shows that there will be some good things happening during this period of unprecedented evil.

Seal Four: Pale Horse and Death (6:7-8)

This horseman is the worse one of all because one quarter of the world's population will be killed. Death will come by war, famine, and even the wild animals, which will be especially hungry due to the scarcity of food. Yet this is only the beginning of woes.

Seal Five: Souls under the Altar and Martyrdom (6:9-11)

These represent believers who are already martyred and will be joined by even more martyrs as the tribulation continues. If the rapture is mid-tribulation or post-tribulation, then their identity is easy to make. But if the rapture is pre-tribulation, then who are these believers? They would be the fruit of the ministry of the 144,000 (Revelation 7 and 14:6-7), or what we call "tribulation saints." So who is persecuting them? It is the great harlot, also known as Ecclesiastical Babylon (Revelation 17:1-6).

Seal Six: Violent Natural Calamities (6:12-17)

To finish off this and the other two major judgements, there will be a series of violent calamities. In the sixth seal, there will be an earthquake, then a major blackout, followed by fallings stars from heaven, which may be a reference to meteors. This meteoric pummelling leads the way to even greater judgements.

Seal Seven: Silence and Seven Trumpets (8:1-2)

This would be a remarkable scene. Christ opens the seventh seal and heaven goes quiet for half an hour—the lull before the storm. Since heaven is not normally a quiet place, this illustrates the great pause before the great blast. Within the seventh seal are the seven trumpet judgements, which are about to begin.

Trumpet One: Hail, Fire and Blood (8:6-7)

This hideous sounding rain will result in trees and green grass being destroyed. One third of the dry land will be un-useable.

Trumpet Two: Great Burning Mountain (8:8-9)

What exactly is this burning mountain? A volcano? While it is not clear, the results of its work will be to destroy one-third of all sea life and ships.

Trumpet Three: Wormwood Star Fall From Heaven (8:10-11)

So far, it has been the seawater that has been affected. Now with the descent of the Wormwood star to earth, one-third of the world's fresh waters will be attacked and destroyed. People will die because this primary source of water will turn bitter. Fruchtenbaum says that "star" refers to angel and Wormwood is a fallen angel who God allows to embitter the world's fresh water so as to fulfil His purpose.[1]

Trumpet Four: Heavenly Bodies Disabled (8:12)

The major sources of light on earth, sun, moon, stars, by day and night, will be struck and one-third will be darkened. It is more likely that it is the light from these heavenly bodies that is hindered, not the actual destruction of these bodies; otherwise our universe would be greatly altered by the departure of these celestial elements.

The Three "Woes"

The three woes are simply the last three trumpet judgements. The flying angel actually says, "Woe, woe, woe to the inhabitants of the earth, because of the remaining blasts of the trumpet of the three angels who are about to sound!" (Revelation 8:13). The fact that each of these trumpets is called "woe" means they will be even more terrifyingly severe than the previous judgements. Some form of announcement of their arrival is made before the judgement begins. Once they come, watch out!

---

[1] Arnold Fruchtenbaum, The Footsteps of the Messiah, Tustin CA: Ariel Press, 1990, page 152.

Trumpet Five or the First Woe: Plague of Locusts (9:1-12)

With the backdrop of the blackout of the fourth trumpet, a terrible event will occur. A fallen star named Abaddon (Hebrew) and Apollyon (Greek), which means "destruction," is introduced. If the "fallen star" mentioned in this passage is actually a demon, then by using the key to the bottomless pit, he is releasing legions of demons to bring judgement on the earth. The bottomless pit is where demons are sent after they have been cast out (Luke 8:31).

As with Hades, the bottomless pit is merely a holding station and not their final abode, which is the lake of fire, prepared for the devil and his angels (Matthew 25:41). Like a prisoner on a day pass, they will be temporarily released to bring judgement on the earth. Their assignment is very focused: do not touch the grass, green things, or trees, but only those people who do not have the seal of God upon them (9:4). Numerous as locusts and painful as scorpions, these demons will have authority to torment, but not kill, impenitent humanity for five months. After the first woe passes, two more will come and take its place.

Trumpet Six or the Second Woe: A Third of Mankind Killed (9:13-20)

This woe will bring a much more severe judgement than the other. Here four fallen angels, not just one, who were bound at the Euphrates River are now released, not for torment, but for murder. One-third of humanity will be destroyed in this woe through plagues. They will spearhead the second

---

[2] See Joel 1:15-2:11 for another description of an end time demonic invasion.

demonic invasion of two hundred million. While some commentators say the two hundred million are Chinese soldiers, the location (Euphrates), their physical description (9:13), and other textual issues preclude these soldiers from being human. The People's Liberation Army (PLA) of the People's Republic of China has no more than four to five million soldiers.

First Half Activities

Remember that while the seven seal and seven trumpet judgements are ensuing, other activities are happening. There is the rise of the 144,000 who will take the everlasting gospel throughout the earth, the ministry of the two witnesses (11:3-6) for three and a half years whose focus is Jerusalem, the political system will be the ten kingdoms and the religious system will be of ecclesiastical Babylon. This is the false, worldwide religious movement which enjoys the support of the civil government (the ten kings). It could even be termed the state religion. Her name is:

> MYSTERY, BABYLON THE GREAT,
> THE MOTHER OF HARLOTS AND OF
> THE ABOMINATIONS OF THE EARTH[3]

Harlotry means unfaithfulness to one's vows, and it can be done in the spiritual realm just like in the physical and marital. Furthermore, this system will trample over true believers and become "drunk on the blood of the saints." Babylon is the birthplace of spiritual adultery through the world's first idolatrous religious system, starting with the rebellious rise of Nimrod (Genesis 10), his building of city states in Mesopotamia, the

---

[3] Revelation 17:5

Tower of Babel (Genesis 11). Now at the end of the age, history goes full circle and returns the one world false religion to the place where it all began.

Mid-Tribulation Events

There is temporary halt to the judgements after the sixth trumpet (second woe). The tribulation reaches half-time. A little book is revealed which gives information on the third woe or the seventh trumpet judgement, which contain all seven bowl judgements. This will a period of intense and dramatic activity, starting with the breaking of the covenant by antichrist and Satan being cast down to earth. Another great war breaks out.

During this period the two witnesses, who have condemned the world through their preaching, are murdered and their lifeless bodies are lying in the streets of Jerusalem. This apparently is the cause of great celebration throughout the world. But after three days the two witnesses rise to life and ascend to heaven for the whole world to see.

Antichrist is killed and rises again thanks to Satan. Three kings are subdued and the other seven submit to antichrist. Ecclesiastical Babylon is destroyed and antichrist worship is set up by the false prophet. At this point the abomination of desolation is set up in the Jerusalem Temple and the infamous "666" mark of the beast is established. Those who refuse to take the mark of the beast or worship the abomination of desolation will be persecuted.

Trumpet Seven or The Third Woe:
The Seven Bowl Judgements (11:14-19; 16:2-21)

Surprisingly there is some very good news preceding the very bad news: the kingdom of this world will now become the Kingdom of Our Lord and of His Christ, Who shall reign forever and ever (11:15). The seventh trumpet/third woe contains the final series of judgements, called the bowl judgements. The purpose is to judge those who are destroying the earth and persecuting the saints. Notice that some of these judgements mirror the plagues that were sent to Pharaoh in the days before the Exodus.

Second Half of the Tribulation

Bowl One: Grievous Sores (16:2)

Those who take the mark of the beast and worship his image will be afflicted with noisome and grievous sores, as predicted in 14:9-11. Though long predicted and well deserved, people will still not repent of their sins, despite the suffering that these sores will bring.

Bowl Two: Sea of blood (16:3)

This bowl pours into the sea and it becomes like a man's blood, so that all that is in the sea dies. The second trumpet caused one third of the sea to turn to blood, this second bowl kills off the remainder of marine life. Things will go from bad to worse.

Bowl Three: Rivers of blood (16:4-7)

This bowl does to the fresh water what the previous one did the seawater: it turns it into blood, killing off the other two-thirds of freshwater life as the third trumpet destroyed one-third. The turning of the freshwater to blood is in retribution for the shedding of the blood of the saints.

Bowl Four: Scorching Sun (16:8-9)

Unlike the fourth trumpet, which diminished the sources of light, the fourth bowl will intensify the heat of the sun so that it scorches unrepentant men. Their response is to blaspheme God, rather than repent. Like Pharoah with a hardened heart, they are being set up for the final denouement.

Bowl Five: Great Darkness (16:10-11)

Another blackout occurs along with an agonizing pain in the mouth, perhaps even biting of the tongue, which causes the blasphemies to rise even higher than before.

The sixth and seventh bowl judgements are related to the events of Armageddon, and will be addressed in our chapter of the Second Coming and the Millennium.

First and Second Half of the Tribulation: A Comparison		
Topic	First Half	Second Half
Political System	Ten Kingdoms	Antichrist's Reign
Religious System	Ecclesiastical Babylon	Beast Worship
Capital	Babylon	Jerusalem

REVIEW QUESTIONS:

1. Name the three types of judgements in Revelation.
2. What does the seventh seal judgement contain?
3. What does the seventh trumpet judgement contain?
4. What are the three "woe's?"
5. What part of the chronology do the two witnesses die and rise again?

Chapter Fifteen

Chronology of Armageddon, the Second Coming, and the Millennium

The most thrilling and exciting prophetic events are contained in this chapter: after a human history full of sin and depravity, culminating in a period of unprecedented evil, God intervenes in the person of Jesus Christ. As a reigning King taking over His rightful domain, Christ will return, establish His everlasting Kingdom, and send His enemies to flight. While there are disagreements as to the timing of the rapture or to the nature of the millennium, all Bible believing Christians can agree that Christ is coming again, He will reign, and we will be with Him forever.

Bowl Six: Euphrates River Dried Up (16:12-16)

The Euphrates is one of the two major rivers of Mesopotamia, which means land between the rivers. On its banks is located the city of Babylon. Antichrist will be gathering the seven remaining submissive kings to join him in an invasion of Israel. The unholy counterfeit trinity is involved in this plot: Satan, the counterfeit father; the beast or antichrist, the counterfeit son; and the false prophet, the counterfeit spirit (16:13); aided and abetted by the spirit of demons.

They will head westward from Babylon to the Central Valley of Israel, known to the world as Armageddon. This famous word comes from the Hebrew *har Megiddo* or "Mountain of Megiddo." Megiddo was a chariot city of Solomon's (I Kings 9:15-19) located in the strategic central valley of Israel, which has five passes. It is the major intersection of the country. The international highway (often called the Via Maris from Isaiah 9:1) comes from Egypt, goes north along the coastal plain, then runs through the Carmel range in the Megiddo pass, crosses the valley, exits into Galilee at the Tabor pass, and onward past the Sea of Galilee to Damascus, Mesopotamia, and the East.

While popular imagination calls Revelation 16:16 the "Battle of Armageddon," there actually is not a battle, in part because there is nothing to battle over. Megiddo is an archaeological site and the only other city in the valley is Afula, which has no strategic value. 16:16 says *"And they gathered them together to the place called in Hebrew Armageddon."*

This verse provides the key: Armageddon is not a battle, but a gathering place for a battle that is to be fought elsewhere. Joel 3:9-11 and Psalm 2:1-6 also describe this future battle. Read Zechariah 12 and 14, for therein lies the ultimate destination of this force: Jerusalem. Remember the analogy from World War II: Southern England was where the Allied troops gathered, but the beaches of Normandy were their destination on D-Day June 6, 1944. We would not say that there was a battle in Southern England, only the place to bring the troops together. The real battle will be elsewhere. For this reason, it is better to call this event the "Campaign of Armageddon," rather than a battle.

Campaign of Armageddon

Babylon Destroyed

There are seven chapters of Scripture that deal with the destruction of Babylon in great detail: Isaiah 13, 14, 47, Jeremiah 50, 51, and Revelation 17, 18. Some of these details clearly could not have happened in history, e.g. destroyed in one day and one hour, the Arabians will not pitch their tents on the site of destroyed Babylon, the heavenly bodies will blacken. Only in the apocalyptic future do they await their future fulfilment. Because of the great evil Babylon has given to the world with cruelty, seduction, violence, and false religion, God will allow it to rise again at the end of the age, so that He can fulfil His prophetic word and live up to His standard of judicial excellence. Babylon will become an economic, political (Zechariah 5:5-11) and religious capital in the last days. While antichrist is focusing on going westward to Armageddon, his enemies will come and destroy his city of Babylon.

Campaign of Armageddon

THE CAMPAIGN OF ARMAGEDDON

VALLEY OF MEGIDDO
(ARMAGEDDON)

MOUNT OF OLIVES

VALLEY OF JEHOSHAPAHT

JERUSALEM

BOZRAH OR PETRA

8 Stages of the Campaign of Armageddon
1. **Gathering of the Armies of Antichrist**
2. **Destruction of Babylon**
3. **Fall of Jerusalem**
4. **Armies of Antichrist at Bozrah**
5. **The National Regeneration of Israel**
6. **The Second Coming of Christ**
7. **Battle at Valley of Jehoshapat**
8. **Victory ascent on the Mount of Olives**

used with permission from: Dr. Arnold Fructenbaum, Ariel Ministries,
www.ariel.org

The Fall of Jerusalem

From the gathering place called Armageddon, antichrist will turn south towards Jerusalem (Zechariah 12:1-3 and 14:1-2). There will be great Jewish resistance (Zechariah 12:4-9 and Micah 4:11-5:1) but eventually the city falls and severe retribution ensues: houses are plundered and the women raped. This successful invasion of the Holy City would seem to spell the end of everything; but it instead sets the stage for the greatest visitation of all time.

Visitation at Bozrah

Now with Jerusalem conquered, the armies of antichrist head to Bozrah in Edom (S.E. Jordan) to deal with the remnant of Jews and Jewish leaders who have fled from Israel (Jeremiah 49:13-14 & Micah 2:12); this is not unlike what happened at the end of the First Jewish Revolt of A.D. 66-70, where after destroying Jerusalem, the Romans went southeast to Masada, just west of the Dead Sea. It was here that the Jewish zealots had their defiant last stand and chose to commit mass suicide rather than surrender to the Romans. The eventual conquest of the stronghold, preceded by the mass suicide of nearly one thousand defenders in A.D. 73, became the material of legend.[1]

As Israel faces this most mortal danger, it will confess its sin and repent over a period of two days (Leviticus 26:40-42; Jeremiah 3:11-18; Hosea 5:15; 6:1-3), then plead for the Messiah to come and save them (Psalm 79:1-13; Psalm 80:1-19; Isaiah 64:1-12; Zechariah 12:10; Matthew 23:37-39) on the third day. Just as the Jewish leaders of Jesus' day led Israel to

---

[1]The site of Masada has become a powerful symbol in modern Israel. Soldiers of the Israel Defense Forces (IDF) are inducted here. "Masada Shall Not Fall Again" has become the motto that testifies of the purposeful survival of the modern reconstituted Jewish state.

reject Messiah, now, after a crushing tribulation, the Jewish leaders of the end-time will lead to the way to His acceptance.

The Apostle Paul told of the longed-for salvation of Israel, saying, "all Israel shall be saved" (Romans 11:25-27). This does not mean every Jew that ever lived, but those Jews who survive the tribulation living in the time of Israel's wholesale national repentance. Jews in Bozrah, Jerusalem, and elsewhere will confess their sins and faith in Messiah concurrently (Zechariah 12:10-13:1; Joel 2:28-32). The results of this will be national conversion and life from the dead (Romans 11:15).

Second Coming of Christ

Popular thought has Christ returning to Jerusalem; in part because it was on the Mount of Olives He ascended (Acts 1:11) and it is the Mount of Olives that His feet shall stand (Zech 14:4). Since the angels said that Christ would return to earth in the same manner as He ascended, it is also assumed that He will return to the same location, too.

Scholars like Arnold Fruchtenbaum propose that Christ will return to Bozrah and offer the following Scriptures:

- **Isaiah 34:1-7:** Bozrah is where the nations will be smitten;

- **Isaiah 63:1-6:** where Isaiah sees a figure coming from Edom glorious in apparel, marching in the greatness of His strength, the One Who speaks in righteousness, mighty to save. His garments are stained in blood because He alone fought a battle to save His people, since there was no one else.

- **Habakkuk 3:3:** says, "*God came from Teman, the Holy One from Mount Paran. Selah*". These geographical locations are in the mountains of Seir and near the site of Bozrah.

- **Micah 2:12-13:** This passage says the remnant of Israel will be gathered like sheep of Bozrah, and their king is passed on before them and Jehovah is at the head of them (the king and Jehovah are the same).

- **Judges 5:4-5:** speaks of the earth trembling when Jehovah goes forth out of Mount Seir and marches in the field of Edom. This, too, is a reference to the vicinity of Bozrah.

How will Christ return[2]?

It is very important that we are clear about this answer. Christ will not quietly return or sneak back to the earth. Matthew 24:30 speaks about Christ coming on the clouds of heaven with power and great glory. The Greek word *parousia* (Greek π α ρ ο υ σ ι α) means "coming" and then subsequent "presence" after coming. Just as Jesus Christ bodily, visibly, and personally ascended to heaven, so He will return in the same manner. It will not be a ghost or wind, but a person in His physical body—a glorified body—but still a human body.

Revelation 19:11-21 speaks of heaven opening up and revealing the Man on a white horse, whose name is called "Word of God," accompanied by the armies of heaven clothed in clean, white fine linen, and the armies of antichrist are destroyed by the sword of his mouth. The battle that commenced at Bozrah will be completed at the Valley of Jehoshaphat near

Jerusalem. Antichrist will be powerfully slain[3] and his army will be routed and destroyed.[4] The bloodletting will be so great that it equals 1,600 furlongs or 320 kilometers by 1 meter high.[5] Birds of the air will have a great feast from the armies of antichrist that are slain.[6] Christ will rule the nations with a rod of iron (Psalm 2:9 and Revelation 19:15).

On His way from Bozrah to Jerusalem, Christ saves the tents of Judah (Zechariah 12:7), fights against the nations who came against Jerusalem (Zechariah 14:3), and then He climbs the Mount of Olives to seal His victory (Zechariah 14:3-4a).

Bowl Seven: Noises, Thunder, Lightning, Earthquake (16:17-21)

This bowl announces the end of the tribulation with the words "*It is done.*" Many cataclysmic events happen with this bowl, including the three fold division of Jerusalem, the final outpouring of wrath on Babylon, the fall of the world's major cities, the destructive outpouring of fifty kilogram hailstones, and the above mentioned noises, thunder, lightning, and earthquakes. Matthew 24:29 and Joel 3:14-17 describe the blackout and earthquake that will happen at this time. With the defeat of the enemy in the Valley of Jehoshaphat and the acclamation of nature, to our relief and joy the tribulation comes to an end.

---

[3] Scriptures about the death of antichrist include Habakkuk 3:13ff; II Thessalonians 2:8; Isaiah 14:3-11;16-21

[4] Destruction of antichrist's army is found in Zechariah 14:12-15; see also Joel 3:12-13.

[5] 320 kilometers is the distance from Eilat/Aqaba on the Red Sea, through the region of Bozrah up to Jerusalem. Whether the blood is all of human or it is simply the product of divine judgement, like turning the sea into blood, remains to be seen.

[6] See also Ezekiel 39:17-29, Revelation 19:17-18, 21 about the feast of the birds.

The Interval

...The demise of the Antichrist and the end of the tribulation will come 1,260 days after the midpoint of the tribulation.

> In this Daniel passage (12:11-12) two other figures are given. The first is 1,290 days, an addition of 30 days during which time the abomination of desolation remains in the temple before its removal. The second figure is 1,335 days, which is 45 days beyond the 1,290 day period and 75 days beyond the 1,260 day period. A special blessing is pronounced on those who will make it to the 1,335th day. The blessing is that those who survive until the 75th day of the interval will enter the messianic kingdom...there will be many who will fail and die before the 1,335th day comes although they did survive past the 1,260th day[7].

It will not be some kind of "long weekend" but a time of needful and intense activity. There will be much clean up to do.

Evil Judged and Removed

The false, unholy trinity will need to be dealt with before entering into a thousand years of righteousness and peace. That old serpent, Satan, is bound up and thrown into the abyss. It is not his permanent abode but will keep him out of the way during the thousand year period (Revelation 20:3).

---

[7]Arnold Fruchtenbaum, The Footsteps of the Messiah, Tustin CA: Ariel Press, 1990, page 256.

As for his evil colleagues, the beast and the false prophet, they are thrown into the lake of fire burning with brimstone (Revelation 19:20). With the elimination of this ungodly trio, it is time to remove the abomination of desolation from its place (Daniel 12:11), which, apparently is not an overnight job.

Judgement

Christ will come and judge the nations (Joel 3:1-3 and Matthew 25:31-46). He will separate them like the shepherd with the sheep versus the goats. The sheep nations, for their kindness to Christ's brethren, will enter into the kingdom with great reward. The goat nations, because of their mistreatment—even persecution—of Christ's brethren, will to condemned into the everlasting fire prepared for the devil and his demons (Matthew 26:41).

While judgement is a very unpopular topic, even in churches, it is the prospect of judgement, with its rewards or retribution, which has and will continue to help people make a qualitative decision of how to spend their lives. God could not be a God of justice without offering His righteous judgement.

Resurrection

The Bible speaks of the "first resurrection," which is also known as the "better" resurrection (Hebrews 11:35). It is this resurrection that every God-fearing person should endeavour to attain (Philippians 3:11). With this resurrection, the righteous will never taste death and live in God's presence forever.

While the dead in Christ will rise at the rapture (I Thessalonians 4:16), the Old Testament righteous (Isaiah 26:19; Daniel 12:2) and the tribulation saints (Revelation 20:4) will rise in the interval period.

Already the hands of the clock are being wound back to the time of the beginning—when God reigned unhindered and everything He made was good.

The Millennium

Just prior to Christ's ascension, His disciples asked Him the question burning on their heart the most: *will you at this time restore the kingdom to Israel?* (Acts 1:6) They had an earthly kingdom in mind, not one in heaven. The Lord did not deny the coming of an (earthly) kingdom but said now was the time to preach the gospel (verses 7 and 8). With the Millennium, the kingdom is restored to Israel--with dividends.

This period is characterized as the earth's Sabbath—where after six days of human misrule, the seventh will be of God's righteous rule through Jesus Christ. He will come and rule from His father David's throne in the City of the Great King, Jerusalem. The hallmarks of His reign will be universal peace (Isaiah 2:4) and universal righteousness (Isaiah 11:3-5). Great topographical changes will happen, with the sweetening of the Dead Sea and the elevation of the Lord's mountain to be higher than any other. Wild animals will become docile, drought will be eliminated except for those who fail to come and worship God in Jerusalem.

Israel will be redeemed in Christ and return to Zion with singing and everlasting joy (Isaiah 35:10; 51:11). It will enter into the New Covenant, restored to the land and every tribe will be given their allotment. The twelve apostles will judge the twelve tribes of Israel (Matthew 19:28).

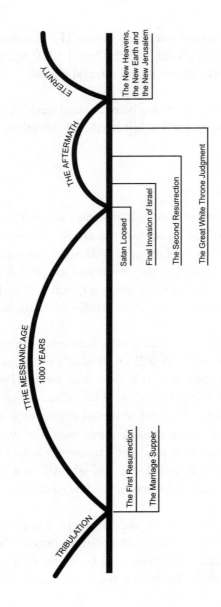

Used with permission from: Dr. Arnold Fruchtenbaum, Ariel Ministries, www.ariel.org

Because the earth shall be filled with the knowledge of the glory of the Lord as the waters cover the sea (Isaiah 11:9), there will be security and material prosperity for all (Micah 4:2-5). The resurrected David will serve as his Son's regent during this period (Jeremiah 30:9; Ezekiel 37:24-25). All outstanding promises of the unconditional theocratic covenants, which have not yet come to pass, will find their fulfilment in the Millennium: Israel's biblical borders, David's restored throne, the provisions of the New Covenant, will all take place.

The Temple will be opened for worship and sacrifice (Ezekiel 37:26-28; 40-46; Zech. 14-16f). Since Ezekiel goes into great detail about this millennial temple, some scholars take it at face value. With this temple will come Sabbaths, oblations, Levitical priesthood, high holidays, and animal sacrifices.

Admittedly, there are problems with this view since Christians understand that Christ is the ultimate sacrifice and there is no need for any more; to have a millennial temple would diminish the finished work of Christ, it is argued. While this author cautions against dogmatism and intolerance of other views, it needs to be remembered that sacrifices can be a memorial. And though it is true that when Jesus died the veil of the temple was rent in two from the top to the bottom, animal sacrifices continued in the Temple for another forty years **after** the crucifixion, only to be discontinued with the latter's destruction. Think about the apostles going to the Temple to pray in the Book of Acts (chapter 3), and they did not seem to cringe that animal sacrifices were still continuing even though Christ proved Himself to be the perfect sacrifice.

The saints will reign with Christ in their resurrected bodies, without limitation.[8] The "sheep nations" join with the redeemed and enter into the Millennium. Under Christ's leadership, justice will be, as it ought to be: crime punished and reduced, oppression halted, law enforcement enhanced, social justice granted, and world peace will reign. The curse of Adam will be reversed (Genesis 3:17) and the earth will be more productive than ever (Isaiah 35:1-2) with more rainfall.

Subjects of the Millennium are Jews and Gentiles who survive the tribulation. They will still be natural people living in mortal bodies, ruled by people with glorified bodies. If this notion seems strange, remember that Jesus Christ, the first fruits from the dead, walked this earth for forty days and nights in a glorified body while fellowshipping with His apostles who had natural bodies.

The natural people will give outward allegiance to Christ and with no Satan to tempt them, sin will be greatly reduced, though not completely eliminated. The Gentiles will go up to Jerusalem to worship God at the Feast of Tabernacles (Zechariah 14:16-17). With Israel evangelizing the world, some of these Gentiles will come to a genuine faith in Christ, while others will not. Satan's temporary post-millennial release will definitely stimulate the rebellious side of the unregenerate millennial subjects.

The thousand year reign of Christ on earth is God's way of honouring His Son in the future for His humiliation in history. The King of Glory will show mankind what a righteous reign really looks like. The Millennium is no democracy—it is a theocracy—but one that is well worth the embrace.

---

[8] Promises of the saints reigning with Christ include Daniel 7:27, Matthew 5:5; II Timothy 2:12; Rev. 2:26-27; the redeemed will serve as administrators and judges in the Millennium Jeremiah 3:15; Daniel 7:18, 27; Luke 19:11-17.

Other Views

Remember that there are two other views embraced by Bible-believing Christians, namely post-millennialism and amillennialism. The former sees the spread of the Gospel and the "Christianizing" of society as bringing in a Golden Age, with the saints ruling and reigning as regents for Christ, who reigns in heaven. Amillennialism offers a simple eschatology: the millennium (and for some, the tribulation) run concurrently with the church age.

For both alternate views, when the age finishes, Christ will return, judge the wicked, reward the righteous and lead them into the Eternal State. Simplified because there are not some of the awkward possibilities that seem possible with premillennialism:

- No need for natural people living side-by-side with people who have glorified bodies;

- Under premillennialism, natural people who survived the tribulation will marry, have sexual relations, and bear children. These people will live and die and some will even sin. Yet the saints, who live and rule among them, have glorified bodies, will not marry or be given to marriage. This seems like an odd arrangement, especially with Christ as King. But this scenario will not occur, of course, under the other two theories.

- No millennial temple with animal sacrifices.

- No need to wait one thousand years for sinless, perfect eternity to emerge. You can have it as soon as Christ returns to earth.

REVIEW QUESTIONS:

1. Though the armies gather at Armageddon, what is the intended target?
2. After the fall of Jerusalem, where does the remnant of Israel take refuge?
3. What is the "Interval Period" and how long is it?
4. What happens to Satan and Antichrist during the Interval?
5. List the four millennial views. Which one do you favour?

Chapter Sixteen

The Eternal State

Arthur Stace (1884-1967) of Sydney Australia had a most unique ministry. He had one sermon that he preached over half a million times. It was not a spoken sermon, nor was it given in a church. Furthermore, it was the world's shortest sermon, consisting of just one word.

Stace gave his sermon, not by mouth, but by hand. He scrawled this single word on the walls and footpaths of Sydney over a period of thirty-seven years. His familiar script was finally patented as a symbol of Sydney's heritage and it graced the famous Harbour Bridge, playfully called "The Coathanger," on 1 January 2000 and at the opening of the Sydney 2000 Olympics. This one-word sermon was called "Eternity."

Our final and long awaited destination is eternity, where the Biblical ideals are fulfilled, our dreams come true, and our longings satisfied. Best of all, we are with God and with each other, in His presence forever and ever. Like the pearl of great price, it is worth off-loading everything else to lay hold of this most important goal. After all, what is the point of obtaining the best this world has to offer and yet miss out on God's eternity? All those riches, fame, and privilege cannot compensate, even a little, for the horrendous loss that awaits those who are estranged from God.

If ever we want people to come out of their parochial, provincial little boxes and take hold of the "big picture" items, then it is time we put eternity before them, the big carrot instead of the little stick. Eternity is God's gift to the redeemed, as hell fire is His destination for the wicked.

Before arriving in Eternity, some post-millennial events need to come to pass. The term for this is:

The Aftermath

The Last Rebellion

After the thousand years are finished Satan will be released from the abyss for a little while (Revelation 20:3). Apart from the length of time in this "little while" is the bigger question of: why is God releasing the enemy of Himself and redeemed humanity after one thousand years of Christ's righteous rule? The simple answer is to purge the world of the last vestiges of sin and rebellion before bringing the perfect realm of eternity to earth.

Satan's release is that he can do one last time that which he does so well: tempt humanity to sin. During the one thousand years, natural people will be under the realm of Christ and give at least nominal allegiance to the One who will rule with a "rod of iron" (Psalm 2:9). On the surface, they will look like acceptable, and accepting, conformists to the will of the King. But the only way to know what is really in the heart of man is through temptation and trials. Those who are truly redeemed will not fall for Satan's ruse, but for the many that are not, he will successfully tempt them to rebel against the Lord. Like a magnetic field, Satan will attract those to himself who have not given a heart allegiance to Christ, whereas the righteous will cleave to Him as the lover of their souls. So with this separation, those who clearly will live with God forever are now set apart from those who do not have redemption in their hearts. The nations will be gathered to battle against the saints by surrounding the beloved city, like a flash flood unexpectedly appearing in the midst of a dry riverbed. But the fire of God will come from heaven and devour them all (Revelation 20:7-9).

The Great White Throne Judgement

11 Then I saw a great white throne and Him who sat on it, from whose face the earth and the heaven fled away. And there was found no place for them.12 And I saw the dead, small and great, standing before God, and books were opened. And another book was opened, which is the Book of Life. And the dead were judged according to their works, by the things which were written in the books.13 The sea gave up the dead who were in it, and Death and Hades delivered up the dead who were in them. And they were judged, each one according to his works.14 Then Death and Hades were cast into the lake of fire. This is the second death.—Revelation 20:11-14

Once Satan's side is routed, then comes the purging. He will be tossed into the lake of fire and brimstone—where the beast and the false prophet were cast over a thousand years earlier—and receive torment day and night forever and ever (verse 10).

Following this the unrighteous dead become part of the second resurrection, which ironically leads to the second death (Rev. 20:13). The sea gives up its dead and death and hades release theirs. Once resurrected, the dead, both small and great, will stand before God at the Great White Throne Judgement. This is the one—and only—time that they will actually have an encounter with the Lord. So awesome and terrifying is this encounter that even the earth and heaven flee away from the brightness of His countenance (Revelation 20:11). The books will be opened and their judgement will be based on the things written in the books.

It appears that all people are written in God's Book (Psalm 139:16). Those who belong to Jesus Christ will not have their name blotted out of God's book (Revelation 3:5) but those who do not know Him will (Exodus 32:32 and Psalm 69:28; see also Revelation 13:8 and 17:8ff, where those who are inclined to worship the beast are lost, since their names are not in the Book of Life).

The "other books" that are opened may very well record the deeds of the lost. If there are "degrees of punishment," as Matthew 11:20-24, Luke 12:47-48, and John 19:11 imply, then it explains the necessity of these other books.

The most important single detail is the ominous sound of Revelation 20:15: *"And anyone not found written in the Book of Life was cast into the lake of fire."* The very place prepared for the devil and his angels is now shared and inhabited with those who did not accept God's gracious offer of eternal salvation through Jesus Christ.

It is not unlike a few of the passengers of the stricken ocean liner Titanic, who refused to get into one of the lifeboats. The result of their decision led them to the bottom of the frigid waters of the North Atlantic. Even more tragic was that some or many of the lifeboats were only half-filled, though there were plenty of passengers thrown into the water. It is a poignant, sobering prospect, out of which can and should serve as a catalyst for evangelism.

In I Corinthians 15:57 it tells *"But thanks be to God, who gives us the victory through our Lord Jesus Christ"*. This passage in essence says it all: that Christ obtained <u>the</u> victory, not just a victory. This is victory over the most ferocious and formidable of adversaries, including Satan, sin, death and hell. Many religions and ideologies have tried to overcome these foes, but in vain.

Christ has overcome them all and as we get to the end of the purging process, these four enemies are dealt a fatal blow. Sin is gone. Satan is cast into the lake of fire. Now, death and hell are also cast into the lake of fire (Rev. 20:14). Christ's victory is complete and He grants us this same victory as we follow after Him.

After defeating the last of all enemies, Christ transfers His authority to the Father, as it says in I Corinthians 15:24-28 (NKJV):

24 Then comes the end, when He delivers the kingdom to God the Father, when He puts an end to all rule and all authority and power.25 For He must reign till He has put all enemies under His feet.26 The last enemy that will be destroyed is death.27 For "He has put all things under His feet." But when He says "all things are put under Him," it is evident that He who put all things under Him is excepted.28 Now when all things are made subject to Him, then the Son Himself will also be subject to Him who put all things under Him, that God may be all in all.

Renovation of Heaven and Earth

The purging of evil process reaches it culmination with the event we call the renovation of the earth. Alluded to in Matthew 24:35; Hebrews 1:10-12; and Revelation 20:11, it is described in detail in II Peter 3:10-13 (NKJV):

10 But the day of the Lord will come as a thief in the night, in which the heavens will pass away with a great noise, and the elements will melt with fervent heat; both the earth and the works that are in it will be burned up.11 Therefore, since all these things will be dissolved, what manner of persons ought you to be in holy conduct and godliness, 12 looking for and hastening the coming of the day of God, because of which the heavens will be dissolved, being on fire, and the elements will melt with fervent heat?13 Nevertheless we, according to His promise, look for new heavens and a new earth in which righteousness dwells.

The old heaven and earth will blaze out of existence and in its place emerges a new heaven and earth, free from the defects, faults, and corruptions inherent in the former fallen order. Like a blazing fire that burns off the dross, so these events will thoroughly cleanse the earth from every bit of sin, iniquity, and rebellion, in order to make room for the prize and place God has prepared for those who love Him (I Corinthians 2:9).

Heaven Comes Down (Revelation 21:1-22:5)

Ponder this for a moment: the Bible was given to show us God's plan to bring us to His Kingdom and Eternity. It is our destination, our goal, and our prize. Yet, the Word of God says relatively little about Eternity, even though it will be the longest and most glorious period of our existence. Indeed, Eternity is 99.99999999999% of our existence, and the earthly life is 0.000000000000000000009%, if that. Yet most of Scripture focuses on the minute fraction of existence called the earthly life, and very little on the main period. Out of 1,189 chapters of the Bible, only one and a quarter are devoted to Eternity (that is one-one thousandth of a percent), or out of 31,214 verses, only thirty-two speak of this subject in one block, with perhaps another eight sprinkled throughout the Bible (same ratio)[1] Why this seeming imbalance?

---

[1] Outside of Revelation 21:1-22:5, there are some very brief allusions to eternity, like in Isaiah 66:22; John 14:1-4; I Corinthians 13:12; II Corinthians 4:17; Colossians 3:4; Galatians 4:26; Hebrews 12.

If the Bible were to describe Eternity, even from a general point of view, imagine the detail that would be involved? And the amount of words it would take to depict it. If the world would have trouble containing an account of **all** the works of Jesus Christ on earth (John 21:25), just imagine how the universe would groan under the weight of the books written about eternity! This is one logical reason why details are sparse.

A second reason is also available. Eternity is when God's plan culminates. Imagine the Lord's ecstasy as He announces, "At last, at last, my plan has been fulfilled, I have redeemed My bride, it is now time to take her into her reward." Like the bridegroom at a wedding, the Lord will sweep up His redeemed into His arms and carry them over the threshold of Eternity, to fulfill and enjoy all that He has planned. And He wants it to be a surprise.

Revelation is a Book About Eternity (Revelation 21:1-22:5)

Back in Chapter Twelve, we discovered five out of six points regarding Revelation. Here is the final point. Revelation is about Eternity. It is here—and only here—that we get a glimpse at that time of unsurpassed shimmering breathless glory, and at least some of our questions begin to find an answer.

Who will be there?

The Triune God, the heavenly hosts, and the redeemed of the Lord will be present.

What will we do in Eternity?

While it is popular to consider that the redeemed go to heaven when they die—which they do, because they go to be with Christ, who dwells in heaven—the fact is that heaven is not our ultimate destination. Some think we will wear damp nighties, floating on clouds, and playing harps. Nowhere does the Scripture hint at such an existence and frankly, would this be an incentive to look forward to eternity? There is much we do not know about the eternal state: what we are going to eat, what we are going to wear, and what we are going to do. Of that, the Bible is silent.

Of course, we can speculate. It will be a time of communion and interaction among the Triune God, the heavenly hosts, and the redeemed. Imagine the thrill of meeting the heroes of faith, face-to-face, as well as Jesus Himself? Will we have visual replays of Biblical and historical events? Will we travel around the universe? Will we be given special missions as we reign with Christ forever? All things are possible.

Where will Eternity Be?

This answer is the easiest. It will be in the New Jerusalem, which descends from heaven and rests on the New Earth. In theory, the New Earth could be larger than the old one; otherwise the size of the New Jerusalem will be all out of proportion to the earth itself.

The city will be a cube of 2,400 kilometers (1,500 miles). The foundations will be twelve layers of precious stones (Revelation 21:19), each having a name of the twelve apostles (21:14). It will be surrounded by a 60 meter (65 yards) high wall, with twelve gates, three on each side, dedicated to the twelve tribes of Israel, made of pearls (hence the phrase, the pearly gates). The streets are made of pure gold like transparent glass. In the midst will be a pure river of the water of life, clear as crystal, with the tree of life in the midst. With brilliant, blinding splendor, the city will not need the sun, for God will provide all the light that is needed.

Now can all of redeemed humanity dwell in this phenomenal city? Dr. Henry Morris, who wrote *The Revelation Record*, speculated on 20 billion redeemed people living in only 25% of the New Jerusalem "cube," since the remainder is public land or royal estate. Adopting his template, this author had one of his eschatology students, who has an engineering background, find out how much land each person could have. They calculated that in 25% of the cube, each individual of the 20 billion redeemed would have a little more than a half cubic kilometer of space each. For most people, that is the biggest block of land they will ever own.

What Will Life Be Like In Eternity?

Many details still wait to be revealed, but these are a sure thing. According to Dwight Pentecost, the Eternal State will have the following:

1. A life of fellowship with Him. I Corinthians 13:12; I John 3:2; John 14:3; Revelation 22:4 and they shall see His face.
2. A life of rest. Revelation 14:13;
3. A life full of knowledge. I Corinthians 13:12 ...*now I know in part; but then shall I know even as also I am known.*
4. A life of holiness Revelation 21:27 *And there shall be no wise enter into it any thing that defileth, neither whatsoever worketh abomination, or maketh a lie; but they which are written in the Lamb's book of life.*

5. A life of joy Revelation 21:4 *And God shall wipe away all tears from their eyes; and there shall be no more death, neither sorrow, nor crying, and there shall there be no more pain; for the former things are passed away.*
6. A life of service. Revelation 22:3 *And there shall be no more curse; but the throne of God and of the Lamb shall be in it; and his servants shall serve him.*
7. A life of abundance. Revelation 21:6 *I will give unto him that is athirst of the fountain of the water of life freely.*
8. A life of glory. 2 Corinthians 4:17 *For our light affliction, which is but for a moment, worketh for us afar more exceeding weight of glory. Colossians 3:4 When Christ, who is our life, shall appear, then shall ye also appear with him in glory.*
9. A life of worship. Revelation 19:1 *And after these things I heard a great voice of much people in heaven, saying, Alleluia; Salvation, and glory, and honour, and power unto the Lord our God. Revelation 7:9–12; Revelation 5:13 Blessing, and honour, and glory, and power*[2].

What Will NOT Be in Eternity?

While it is desirable, even somewhat needful, to know what and who will be in eternity, it remarkable to note that God defines this state of endless life not by the things that are in, but by those very things that are not in it.

Eighteen things, seventeen that are present today, will not be present in eternity. For the most part, we will be very glad to say good-bye to these things. Since Jesus Christ gives us "the victory," this also translates into the elimination of these items which have hemmed in and harmed

---

[2] Dwight Pentecost, Things to Come, Grand Rapids: Zondervan, 1964, page 581.

humankind since the beginning. Some of the items are not necessarily evil in themselves, but even their loss is merely because God wants to replace them with something better.

In Eternity, there will be no more...

1. **Death (20:14; 21:4):** This is the last and greatest of enemies, the grim reaper that never discriminates but devours all sooner or later. While God has turned this enemy into the catalyst of catapulting His saints into glory, it must and will be eliminated. It came as a result of paradise lost, and it will be cast into the lake of fire as paradise is regained.

2. **Hades (20:14):** The grave and underworld, the dim joyless place of departed spirits, will be emptied and then destroyed. Memories of standing by a gravesite weeping uncontrollably will be a thing of the past as Hades takes its place in the lake of fire.

3. **Sea (21:1):** The Sea is not necessarily an evil thing, but Israel was not a maritime nation and it was the affairs of the land to which it revolved. In addition, the sea represented the oppressive heathen beyond the waters, particularly the Philistines from Caphtor, Greece and the Hellenistic empire, and the might of Rome itself. The image of the beast coming out of the sea (Rev. 13:1) again gives this a negative connotation in Hebrew thought. In essence, the sea separates people but under Christ in eternity, all the redeemed from all nations and ages will be brought together and made as one, never to separate again.

4. **Sorrow (21:4):** Like the first two items, sorrow is a result of the fall and represents our cursed existence. It is the common human condition and few can escape. Yet the time is coming when sorrow will also be tossed out. God will wipe away every tear from our eyes. Joy will completely and permanently supplant this curse.

5. **Crying (21:4):** While there is such a thing as "crying for joy," admittedly most crying in the world is due to sorrow. When sorrow flees away, the crying will go with it.

6. **Pain (21:4):** Also part of the curse given at the Fall, pain is so universal. It is a difficult taskmaster. Yet pain will also disappear in the light of the New Jerusalem.

7. **Cowardly (21:8):** Cowardice is a common as courage is rare, not unlike lying versus truth. Even the attitude of bullying and intimidation is one of the highest signs of cowardice. It was through cowardice that Joseph's brothers betrayed him, and Potiphar's wife delivered him to the prison. Cowardice caused Herod to behead John the Baptist, the disciples to flee at the Garden of Gethsemane, as well as the Asian believers during Paul's first hearing (II Timothy 4:16). But righteousness and the Holy Spirit bring great boldness in this day, and these things will deliver us to the kingdom where the day never ends.

8. **Unbelieving (21:8):** Of the myriad of sins found in the world, none is worse than the evil heart of unbelief (Hebrews 3:12); after all, a person can be forgiven of any sin, but there is no forgiveness when unbelief persists. Israel tempted God ten times (Numbers 14:22), and rotted in the wilderness as a result. Unbelief has been the universal bar from

entering into a new life in Christ. This greatest of all impediments will be purged out of the universe when the new heavens and new earth come to us.

9. **Abominable (21:8):** The tribulation will be replete with abominations, though these things will hardly be new. The offensive, defiant, objectionable, and unspeakable, will all be bundled up and thrown away forever in the light of eternity.

10. **Murderers (21:8):** Killers and haters are all the same in God's sight (Matthew 5:22); out of satanically-tainted, flesh-filled spite they lash out to hurt and destroy. God's nature is to love, create, and build up. Only when murderers are driven out of the universe can the innocent blood be vindicated and the light will shine brightest.

11. **Sexually immoral (21:8):** It may not be either well-known or well-received, but sexual sin is worse than other sins. Yes, all sins can earn the individual the same wages, which is death. But sexual sin is especially repugnant because it is a sin against God (Genesis 39:9), against his or her own body, and against a person's future or present family. Immorality is very bad for family health and stability, and is especially abhorrent in the sight of God. While society may condone extramarital "sexploits," God never will and the time is coming that these will be tolerated no longer. The sexually immoral will be "outside" the walls of the city, a euphemism for the lake of fire. Moral purity will reign forever.

12. **Sorcerers (21:8):** This is based on rebellion against God and partnering with evil spirits. The cocktail this produces is explosive beyond words. All these things will find their final abode with the devil and his angels.

13. **Idolaters (21:8):** Though a clear violation of the second commandment, idolatry has been present before and very much after the time of Moses. Idolatry worships the creation rather than the creator, and today's materialism is taking its rightful place in the totem pole of idolatrous practices. All these things will be banished when Eternity comes.

14. **All liars (21:8):** Satan is a liar and the father of lies (John 8:44). Lying is his mother tongue. Any coward can and does lie, but it takes courage and strength to remain faithful to the truth, even when it hurts. Christ is truth, the Gospel is truth, and all those who live for Him will live and give of the truth. These are the things that lead to eternal life. Thank God, lying will be gone for good.

15. **Temple (21:22):** It is hard for us to miss a Temple that has not been around for nearly two millennia, but God does not need it for sacrifice or for His abode. The New Jerusalem will be one big Temple of God.

16. **Night (21:25):** Night is associated with time and also evil. We have been limited by time and oppressed by that which is done at night. When we enter into that pristine pure period where evil is history, day and night will cease and God's Shekinah glory will light our way. Time will reign no more and God will reign forever.

17. **Curse (22:3):** The first sin of the first parents brought the fall of mankind and with it, a curse. All the evil, calamities, tragedies, and broken dreams are a direct result of the curse. But this enemy will also be defeated and blessing shall overwrite and overcome in all areas.

18. **Dogs (22:15)**: For many dog-lovers, this is a note of great sadness. While it can be used of real dogs, *kuon* it also has a metaphorical sense of intense moral impurity that will bar an individual from eternity. The Jews used this term to describe the Gentiles, especially due to the lack of circumcision and ceremonial impurity. It would appear that in Revelation it also has a metaphorical sense of applying to all of the above type of people who loved their sin rather than God.

The fact that eternity will be free of these things should make it all the more wonderful and attractive. It will be the best eternal home imaginable. As Paul said, *For I consider that the sufferings of this present time are not worthy to be compared with the glory which shall be revealed in us* (Romans 8:18).

The glory of eternity will give us wonderful amnesia to the pain and poverty of the past in order to focus on the bliss, blessing, and beauty of that time when day and night cease.

Aren't you glad you serve such a God of glory?

Paradise Lost and Paradise Regained: Genesis and Revelation Contrasted	
Probationary World (Genesis)	**Eternal State (Revelation)**
Division of light & darkness (1:4)	No night there (21:25)
Division of land & sea (1:10)	No more sea (21:1)
Rule of sun & moon (1:16)	No need of sun & moon (21:23)
Man in a prepared garden (2:8,9)	Man in a prepared city (21:2)
River flowing out of Eden (2:10)	River flowing from God's Throne (22:1)
Gold in the land (2:12)	Gold in the city (21:21)

Paradise Lost and Paradise Regained: Genesis and Revelation Contrasted	
Probationary World (Genesis)	**Eternal State (Revelation)**
Tree of life in the midst of the garden (2:9)	Tree of life throughout the city (22:2)
Bdellium & onyx stone (2:12)	All manner of precious stones (21:19)
God walking in the garden (3:8)	God dwelling with His people (21:3)
Cursed ground (3:17)	No more curse (22:3)
Daily sorrow (3:17)	No more sorrow (21:4)
Thorns and thistles (3:18)	No more pain (21:4)
Sweat on the face (3:19)	Tears wiped away (21:4)
Eating herbs of the field (3:18)	Twelve manner of fruits (22:2)
Returning to the dust (3:19)	No more death (21:4)
Evil continually (6:5)	Nothing that defiles (21:27)
Coats of skins (3:21)	Fine linen, white & clean (19:14)
Satan opposing (3:15)	Satan banished (20:10)
Kept from the Tree of Life (3:24)	Access to the Tree of Life (22:14)
Banished from the garden (3:23)	Free entry to the city (22:14)
Redeemer promised (3:15)	Redemption accomplished (5:9,10)

REVIEW QUESTIONS:

1. What are two reasons why God does not tell us in the Bible about Eternity?
2. Where will Eternity be located?
3. How many things will not be in Eternity, as listed in the Bible?

Chapter Seventeen

A Glossary of Key Terms

A student of Eschatology is a candidate for a great adventure. It will bring insight, anticipation, and even excitement to his or her perspective. But in order to understand this subject for what it is, such a student needs to learn a new vocabulary. Defining key terms is vital for getting a handle of this crucial subject.

Abomination of Desolation: This event is the horrifying defilement of God's Holy Place. It is referred to six times in Scripture (Daniel 9:27; 12:11; Matthew 24:15; Mark 13:14; II Thessalonians 2:3-4; Revelation 13:15). Prophesied in the Book of Daniel, it refers to an event of the past (Daniel 11:31) as well as the future.

Historically, the Seleucid Syrian Ruler Antiochus IV, also known as "Antiochus Epiphanes" or "God-manifest," went to the Jewish Temple in Jerusalem in the year 168 B.C. and sacrificed a pig to the god Zeus on the high altar. This horrendous sacrilege precipitated what became known as the Maccabean Revolt, which successfully ejected the Seleucids from the Temple, Jerusalem, and Israel. You can read more of this incident in the apocryphal book of I Maccabees 1:54ff.

Two hundred years later, Jesus Christ speaks about a future event in Matthew 24:15 and Mark 13:14 that will herald the final stage of the Great Tribulation and culminate in the Second Coming of Christ. People who know about and observe this event will understand that Christ's return is very soon. A literal understanding of these verses means the final "Abomination of Desolation" will happen in the Tribulation period when a Third Temple is built and the False Prophet, acting on behalf of the Antichrist, sets up his image in the Holy of Holies, thus defiling the Temple and declaring himself to be God (II Thessalonians 2:3-4; Rev 13:14-15). This event signals the half-way mark of the Tribulation and unleashes the wrath of God. Remember that not all scholars accept such a literal interpretation.

Abrahamic Covenant: Demy and Ice call this "the mother of all redemptive covenants." The Abrahamic Covenant is based on Genesis 12:1-3 where God unconditionally promises the patriarch Abraham three vital things: a) the land of Canaan, which is amplified in the Palestinian Covenant (Deut. 30); seed or posterity, amplified in the Davidic Covenant (II Samuel 7); and universal blessing, as fulfilled in the New Covenant (Jeremiah 31). It is impossible to understand or appreciate Eschatology without knowledge of the redemptive Biblical covenants.

Age: Derived from the Greek words aion and aionios, age speaks of "periods of time." This can be a period of time yesterday, today, tomorrow, or for all time. Redemption in Christ ultimately leads us from the time-bound realm of the age into eternity where time has no meaning at all—day and night, spring and summer, today, tomorrow, and forever, are all the same. The Hebrew word olam means "long duration, antiquity, futurity" and is translated as "eternal." Christ promises His disciple-making followers that He will be with them always, even to the end of the (present) age (Matthew 28:20).

Allegorical Interpretation: This method gives a different, hidden, and supposedly superior interpretation to a text. The idea is that the true meaning of the text is hidden underneath the plain meaning.

Amillennialism: One of the major views of Bible prophecy. It teaches that there will not be a literal thousand year millennial reign of Christ, as mentioned in Revelation 20; instead the church age becomes the millennium where believers reign on earth and Christ reigns in heaven.

Antichrist: (Greek Antichristos): One of the most famous, ferocious and formidable characters in Bible prophecy. The term is used four times in four verses, all in John's minor epistles (I John 2:18, 22; 4:3 and II John 1:7), but he is alluded to in both testaments, especially in Daniel and its New Testament companion, Revelation. "Antichrist" means "against Christ" and also "in the place of Christ." He will be the last great enemy Christ overcomes during the Great Tribulation and also symbolizes the last great world rebellion before Christ returns.

Armageddon: This is the last great military campaign of human history, described in Daniel 11:40-45; Joel 3:9-17; Zechariah 14:1-3; and Revelation 16:14-16. It is derived from the Hebrew term Har meaning "mountain" and Megeddon from "Megiddo," a chariot city in the Central Valley of Israel. Since Megiddo is basically an archaeological site today, it is more likely that the Campaign of Armageddon has another intended destination. That would be Jerusalem. An analogy would be from the 1944 Allied D-Day Invasion of Nazi-occupied Europe: the "gathering place" of the Allied Troops was southern England, whereas the destination was the coastline of Normandy in France.

Babylon: The greatest city of the ancient world, Babylon was built on the banks of the Euphrates River in the land of Shinar, in what is now known as Iraq. The builder of Babylon is traditionally considered to be Nimrod in Genesis 10. Babylon became especially famous during the Second Babylonian Empire of Nebuchadnezzar (605-562 B.C.), as described in Daniel Chapters 2 to 4. The city symbolizes the best humankind offers (humanism). But its notoriety comes from its renowned spirit of rebellion against the Living God, as typified by the hasty building of the Tower of Babel (Genesis 11) and as the birthplace of heathenism.

After Daniel's day, the city gradually declined in importance until it basically disappeared under the Mesopotamian dust just before the arrival of Islam in the seventh century A.D. The Muslims, under the Abbasid Empire, were forced to start a new capital city called Baghdad on the Tigris (A.D. 750).

The city was reconstructed in the days of Saddam Hussein in the 1980's. It has become known as the "City of Satan" as Jerusalem is known as the "City of God." Seven chapters are devoted to the fall of Babylon (Isaiah 13, 14, 47, Jeremiah 50, 51, Revelation 17 and 18).

Beast: The most common Bible name for the one called "Antichrist." The term is used 25 times in the Book of Revelation.

Blessed Hope: Used in Titus 2:13, it refers to the coming of Jesus Christ for His saints. When Christ returns, the saints will receive sinless resurrected bodies and enter into the ultimate stage of redemption named "glorification."

Book of Life: Mentioned nine times in Scripture (Exodus 32:32-33; Psalm 69:28; Philippians 4:3; Revelation 3:5; 13:18; 17:8; 20:12,15; 21:27), where God records the names of the righteous. Only believers in Jesus Christ are found written in the Book of Life. According to Revelation 20:11-12, the Book of Life will be open at the Great White Throne Judgement. All people whose names are not found in the Book of Life will be cast into the lake of fire.

Bottomless Pit: Known as the abyss, this is the holding place of those whose ultimate abode will be the lake of fire. The term is used seven times in the Book of Revelation (9:1, 2, 11; 11:7; 17:8; 20:1, 3). Satan will be housed here during the Millennium.

Bowl Judgements: The third of the three series of judgements. Each judgement has seven judgements. The bowl judgements are the worse of all and are a well-deserved response to all the sins of the tribulation, culminating in the abomination of desolation. Its final manifestation (Rev. 16:17-21) is a great earthquake, flashes of lightning, and hailstones, which herald the Second Coming of Christ.

Bozrah: Located in the area of Mount Seir in South West Jordan, it is traditionally considered to be at the historic site of the rose-red city of Petra. Bozrah is where the Jewish remnant will flee in the middle of the Tribulation from the wrath of Antichrist (Matthew 24:15-21 and Revelation 12:6,14). Antichrist will attack the Jews in Bozrah (Jeremiah 49:13,14) and they will plead for the Messiah to come and rescue them (Hosea 6:1-3). Messiah will come and rescue His people from Bozrah and then have a victory ascent on the Mount of Olives (Zech. 14:4).

Chiliasm: derived from the Greek word for 1,000, chiliasm is the ancient label for what we call "The Millennium" or the thousand year reign of Christ.

Church Age: traditionalists define this as the period from the Day of Pentecost, when the church was born, until the Rapture of the Church. Apart from these two events, the church age is not specifically alluded to in end-time prophecy.

Covenants: Derived from the Hebrew word brit and Greek word diatheke, it stands for a binding agreement between two parties. If adhered to, all parties stand to gain greatly. If broken, there are severe consequences. Theocratic covenants of the Bible refer to God's dealings with His people. It is impossible to understand eschatology without some background in covenants.

Covenant Theology: This is a system of theology, not based on Biblical covenants, but on two abstract covenants that help systematize salvation's history. Covenant of Works deals with God and Adam. Covenant of Grace is between God, Christ and Christian believers.

Daniel's Seventy Weeks: Based on Daniel 9:24-27, it defines the prophetic events that lead to the crucifixion of Christ and Great Tribulation. It is the foundation of all end-time prophecy. The Seventieth Week, or the Last Week, is synonymous with the Great Tribulation. It is from this Seventieth Week in Daniel, not the Book of Revelation that we get the notion of a seven year Great Tribulation.

Davidic Covenant: This was made between God and David (II Samuel 7:4-17 & I Chronicles 17:10-15), whereby God promises David an everlasting dynasty and throne. According to I Chronicles 17, Messiah will come from the seed of David and his house, throne, and kingdom will last forever.

Day of the Lord: Not a literal twenty-four hour day, this term refers to the travail pains and birth of the coming Kingdom. The Tribulation and Millennium periods would constitute the major components of the Day of the Lord.

Dispensationalism: This teaching takes all of God's dealings in human history and divides it into seven dispensations. It is based on literal interpretation of prophecy and makes a distinction between God's plan for Israel and the Church. It was popularized by John Nelson Darby (1800-1882) and the Scofield Reference Bible. The seven dispensations are:

1. Dispensation of Innocence (Genesis 2-3);
2. Dispensation of Conscience (Genesis 4-6);
3. Dispensation of Government (Genesis 10-11);
4. Dispensation of Promise (Genesis 12-50);
5. Dispensation of Law (Exodus 1- Acts 1; Matthew 11:13);
6. Dispensation of the Church (Ephesians 3:1-10; Romans 11:1-27); Great Tribulation (Revelation 11:1-3; Matthew 24:21; Daniel 9:24-27); and
7. The Millennium (Revelation 20:1-10; Isaiah 60:1-22).

Dominion: a modern form of postmillennialism that takes its name from God's command for mankind to take dominion over creation. It believes that a Golden Age of Godliness will precede the Second Coming of Jesus. It is a form of Christian nationalism that espouses a theocratic or theonomic government. There is a link between dominionists, reconstructionists, and Kingdom Now.

Eisegesis: From the Greek meaning to "lead into" or "introduce into". The Merriam Webster Online dictionary defines it as the interpretation of a text (as of the Bible) by reading into it one's own ideas.[1] It is where the individual inserts or splices his or her own ideas into the Biblical text. Eisegesis is considered poor exegesis and is to be avoided.

End: As the study of "last things," eschatology deals with the period of human history known as "The End." Two Greek words help us understand this concept.

Eschatos (Greek means "end" in position, time, space).
- "The first shall be ESCHATOI (last ones)"— Matthew 19:30
- "Unto the ESCHATOU (last part) of the earth" — Acts 1:8
- "Children, it is the ESCHATE hour."— I John 2:18
- It is this word that has given us *Eschatology*.

Telos (Greek τ ε λ ο ς end, completion, goal)
- "Christ is the TELOS of the law"—Romans 10:4. This word does not mean destruction, but fulfilment of purpose.
- "And if Satan has risen up against himself and is divided, he cannot stand, but is coming to TELOS" (no longer exists) — Mark 3:26

---

[1] http://www.m-w.com/cgi-bin/dictionary?book=Dictionary&va=eisegesis

- "The end (TELOS) of the commandment is love" (outcome, results, goal).
- In some ways, it would be more appropriate to refer to Eschatology as Teleology, because in the end God's purposes will be fulfilled to the letter.

Eternal State: Mostly described in Revelation 21:1-22:5, it is that blessed period known as "forever and ever" where redeemed humanity will live with God and His heavenly hosts in the New Jerusalem.

Exegesis: From the Greek "to explain" or "interpret," exegesis seeks to draw meaning out of the text (like hot water in a cup draws flavour and color from the tea bag). It takes into account the key words of the text, historical and cultural background, limits of the passage, and context within the text. Good exegesis should be the goal of every Bible student.

Four Horsemen of the Apocalypse: These are the first four seals of the Seal Judgements, described in Revelation 6:1-8, with various riders on four differently coloured horses.

Futurism: One of the four interpretive views that says that Bible prophecy, especially everything after Revelation 4, will occur in the future.

Gehenna: (Greek geenna) Originally this term referred to the Valley of the Sons of Hinnom to the west of the Old City of Jerusalem, next door to Mount Zion, that has become the symbol of eternal punishment. Originally the municipal rubbish tip and location of fiery sacrifice of infants (II Kings 16:3; 21:6), Jeremiah pronounced it as a place of divine judgement (7:32; 19:6). It is alluded to in the very last verse of the Book of Isaiah (66:24).

Jesus refers to this place in Mark 9:43-48 when He speaks about the place where the fire is not quenched and the worm never dies

Gog and Magog: The prophecy of Ezekiel chapters 38 and 39 describes a great, unexpected, and unprovoked invasion of Israel in the latter days. "Magog" means "from Gog," so literally the phrase "Gog and Magog" means "Gog from (the Land of) Gog." The invader will be Gog and a coalition of nations. They meet a disastrous end when God intervenes from heaven. Many interpret Gog to be Russia, Persia as Iran, Phut as Libya, and Cush as Ethiopia/Sudan. Of interest is that no Arab neighbour of Israel is mentioned as part of the warring coalition. This term has become synonymous with anti-God or anti-christ forces throughout history, though the literal fulfilment of this prophecy is yet to come.

Great Tribulation: Known also as "Daniel's Seventieth Week," it refers to the seven year period at the end of the age when the forces of evil, lead by antichrist and the false prophet, make their last stand before their complete overthrow by Christ at His Second Coming. Some label the last three and a half years, after the abomination of desolation and during the outpouring of divine wrath, to be the "Great" Tribulation or the "Greater Tribulation" versus the lesser one in the first three and a half years.

Great White Throne Judgement: Recorded in Revelation 20:11-15, this speaks about the judgement of the dead after the Millennium. All are judged according to their works. Whoever is not found written in the Book of Life will be cast into the lake of fire.

Hades: Used 11 times in the NKJV. The Greek equivalent to the Hebrew *sheol,* Hades is the dim and dreadful underworld location where the departed spirits and a dour Greek mythological god live. It is a place of punishment (Matthew 11:23; Luke 10:15; 16:23). Hades can also mean the state of death after the earthly life (Matthew 16:18; Acts 2:27, 31; Revelation 1:18; 6:8; 20:13, 14). The occupants of Hades do not stay there permanently; their final destination is the lake of fire after the great white throne judgement.

Harlot: The harlot is the bride of Satan just as the church is the bride of Christ. It represents false religious systems from the Tower of Babel of Genesis 11 to Revelation 17. She will be used to seduce people to follow the beast and Satan. The harlot will martyr true believers. Eventually, the beast will tire of her and destroy her (Revelation 17:16).

Heaven: The word occurs 582 times in the English Bible.[2] It comes from the Hebrew word shamayim "the heights" or Greek ouranos that which is raised up." There is a three-fold division of heaven: the first or atmospheric heaven; the second or celestial heaven; nd the third heaven, where God lives.

Hell: From the Greek word Gehenna geenna (see above); hell is the place of permanent separation from the living God and eternal punishment. Two strong New Testament passages on the subject are Matthew 25:41, 46 and II Thessalonians 1:9. The word "hell" is found 54 times in the KJV and 32 times in the NKJV.

Historical Context: In order to better understand prophetic passages, the Bible student should know the historical context. This includes knowledge of history, geography, culture, politics of the day, as well as the reason the author wrote the book, if this is mentioned. Good study Bibles and other reference helps can provide this important information.

---

[2] The word "heavens" is found 133 times.

Historicism: One of four views that seeks to answer the question, when in history will prophecy be (or was) fulfilled. The other views are idealism, futurism, and preterism. It takes the events of Revelation chapters 4 through 19 and gradually fulfils them throughout the whole of the church age. Some historicists adopt the day/year theory, meaning a mention of days e.g. 2,300 days of Daniel 8:14 will actually be years. This view was popular with Protestant reformers and also reconstructionists.

Idealism: Another one of the four views that seeks to answer when prophecy will be fulfilled. Very similar to historicism in that it takes the events of Revelation chapters 4 through 19 and stretches them throughout all of church history. However, these events are not time-pegged at all but symbolically represent the great truths of God. The application of these truths is timeless. Liberal theologians are among those who favour this view.

Imminence: The doctrine that teaches Jesus Christ could come back for His saints in the rapture at any moment, without the prior fulfilling of prophetic signs. Christ's "imminent" return is the hope of every true believer. It is the hallmark of the pre-tribulation rapture theory .

Intermediate State: That part of human existence between physical death and physical resurrection. The saints are with the Lord in heaven and the sinners are in hades.

Interval Period: This is the period described in Daniel 12:11-12 and elsewhere between the Second Coming of Christ and the start of the Millennium.

Israel: This name can mean a) Jacob; b) sons of Jacob; c) the people of God; d) a kingdom in Canaan; e) a modern nation-state in Palestine. Bible prophecy affects three groups of people: Israel, the Gentiles or nations, and the Church. Israel has a prominent role in God's prophetic plan, if you take the prophetic passages literally. Daniel's Seventy Week prophecy is meant to be for Israel and Jerusalem (9:24).

Jerusalem: The most famous city of the Bible, mentioned 822 times in 771 verses. In ancient times, it was Israel's holy city and capital since the time of David and made special by God for the King's sake. Place were Christ was crucified and resurrected. The city has become sacred to Christians and Muslims and possesses some of the most sacred holy sites in the world. Zechariah 12 predicts the city will be the scene of great worldwide controversy and conflict in the end times. Slated to be Christ's capital during the millennium, it is also the name of the heavenly city where the righteous will dwell in the Eternal State.

Jews: Originally these were Israelites from the tribe of Judah alone. After the Babylonian captivity this term has come to describe any individual from any of the twelve tribes of Israel. It means a Hebrew or Israelite.

Judgements: The Bible describes several judgements. For the unbelievers, these include the seven seal, trumpet, and bowl judgements, as well as the great white throne judgement of Revelation. For believers, there is the Judgement Seat of Christ (Romans 14:10 and II Corinthians 5:10), where we receive rewards for the deeds done in the body.

Kingdom: There are several descriptions of "kingdom" in Scripture where each speak of a king, subjects, and a realm. These include: a) David's

Kingdom, the fulfilment of the Davidic covenant which will occur in the Millennium; b) universal kingdom, representing God's rule in the world; c) the spiritual kingdom, God's rule over His people at all times; d) the mystery kingdom, which is equivalent to the church age (between the two comings of Christ); e) the kingdom of man, the (rebellious) reign of humanity since the Tower of Babel which will eventually be overthrown at the Second Coming of Christ; f) the kingdom of God, which popularly means Christ's millennial reign.

Kingdom Now: A theological belief similar in some ways to Reconstructionism, it has a following among a few Pentecostal and charismatics. It believes that God lost control of the world at The Fall and is regaining it through His covenant people who, through ministry and social action, bring the kingdom of Christ now. Reconstructionists are Calvinist, teach theonomy (the continued validity of the Old Testament), and cessationism, namely the gifts of the Spirit ceased in the first century. The election of US President George W. Bush and his first-term Attorney General John Ashcroft, both devout Christians, was viewed by some Kingdom Now advocates as a vindication of their cause in the public square; however, their theology has never been endorsed publicly by any politician.

Lake of Fire: The final abode of the ungodly. Mentioned five times in Scripture, all in Revelation (19:20; 20:10, 14, 15; 21:18), unbelievers will be cast there after the great white throne judgement. At present, no one is in the lake of fire, but chronologically, the beast and false prophet will go there after the Tribulation. Satan and the unbelievers will go there after the Millennium.

Literal Interpretation: The preferred method of Bible interpretation where the plain meaning of Scripture is the first consideration. Issues of historical, cultural, and political context are considered. It has been said that when the plain sense makes sense, seek no other sense, otherwise you will have nonsense.

Mark of the Beast: Found in Revelation 13:16, 17; 14:9; 20:4, this is the brand or "tattoo" on individuals who are followers of the Beast and Satan. No one will be able to buy or sell without the mark and those who refuse it will be persecuted.

Marriage of the Lamb: Christ will marry the church, according to Ephesians 5:25-32. After the rapture, the church in heaven will prepare for her marriage by adorning herself with white linen garments, which are the righteous acts of the saints (Revelation 19:8). These garments are received at the Judgement Seat of Christ, according to their works. So the church is presented to Christ in heaven, and as Revelation 19:7ff says "... *for the marriage of the Lamb has come and His bride has made herself ready.*"

Marriage Supper of the Lamb: Found in Revelation 19:9, this supper is akin to a reception after a wedding. Though the marriage of the Lamb is in heaven, the marriage supper occurs here on earth. Some say this supper will happen the Interval Period between the second coming and the millennium (Daniel 12:11-12), but it may also occur in the Millennium (Luke 22:18).

Messianic Kingdom: This kingdom is what the prophets of Israel longed for. Some major passages include Psalm 15 and 24; Isaiah 2:2-3; 11:6-9;

65:17-25; Micah 4:1-5. The Messiah will come and rule from David's throne in Jerusalem. Synonymous terms include the Davidic kingdom, the Millennium, and the Kingdom of God.

Midtribulation Rapture Theory: This teaches that the rapture of the church occurs in the middle of the tribulation period, at the time that the Abomination of Desolation is set up.

Millennium: Latin is *mille anum* or one thousand years. This is a literal thousand year period where Jesus Christ rules on the throne of David in Jerusalem after His Second Coming. It is the period of history where any outstanding prophecies or covenantal promises will be fulfilled.

Narratives: Narratives are stories, though unlike stories that have the connotation of being fictitious like a bedtime story; narratives constitute forty percent of Scripture. Daniel is considered narrative and large parts of Ezekiel are, too, even though they are major prophetical books.

Nebuchadnezzar's Statue: Found in Daniel 2, this statue was revealed in a dream to Nebuchadnezzar, King of Babylon. It outlines the period called the "times of the Gentiles" all the way to the Second Coming of Christ and the Millennial Kingdom. Four Gentile kingdoms will arise in that day, including Babylon the Head of Gold, Persia the chest and arms of silver, Greece the belly and thigh of bronze, and Imperial Rome the legs of iron, feet of iron and clay. This four part statue will be destroyed by the stone cut without hands, which represents God's never-ending kingdom.

New Covenant: This covenant fulfils the "blessing" aspect of the Abrahamic covenant, especially regarding salvation (Jeremiah 31:31-37; 32:40; Isaiah

55:3; 59:21; 61:8-9; Ezekiel 16:60; 34:25-31; 37:26-28; Romans 11:25-27; Hebrews 8:7-9:1; 10:16-17). The New Covenant was made with Israel but the church does participate in the spiritual blessings of the covenant; in fact, it is by this covenant that we receive salvation in Christ.

New Heaven and New Earth: After the Millennium, the first heaven and earth pass away (II Peter 3:10-12 & Revelation 22:3) and a new heaven and earth emerge. We have very little information about either, though some commentators say the new earth is equivalent to the New Jerusalem and the New Heaven will neither have sun or stars, since God Himself will be the light (Revelation 21:23-25; 22:5).

New Jerusalem: Using the name "Jerusalem," in association with David, his covenant, and the City of the Great King, this eternal city will come from heaven and be the dwelling place of God, His heavenly hosts, and His redeemed for ever. It is described as a cube 2,400 kilometers in dimension. God, the heavenly hosts, and all God's redeemed people will dwell in the New Jerusalem forever and ever.

Olivet Discourse: Just before His crucifixion, Jesus Christ gave this final public discourse on the Mount of Olives, which is just east of Jerusalem. Found in Matthew 24-25; Mark 13; and Luke 17:20-37; 21:5-36, it speaks of end-time events and parallels events in Zechariah 12-14 and Revelation 6-19. Many commentators believe the discourse pertains to Israel, especially with references to the abomination of desolation or pray you do not have to flee on the Sabbath day.

Palestinian Covenant: Found in Deuteronomy 29:1-30:10, it covers the "land" aspect of the Abrahamic covenant. It basically grants the land of

Canaan to the descendants of Abraham via Isaac, namely the Jews (30:5). They will not always live there throughout history but eventually they will return there permanently. Some have used this covenant to justify the creation of the State of Israel in 1948.

Partial Rapture Theory: Doctrine that says the rapture will be pretribulational but only spiritual Christians will go up. Carnal Christians will remain on earth to be purified during the coming Tribulation.

Postmillennialism: The Church will conquer, dominate, and Christianize the world, thus ushering in the visible Kingdom before the Second Coming of Christ. When the Church has fulfilled this task, then Jesus will return.

Posttribulation Rapture Theory: This theory teaches that all Christians will be raptured after the Great Tribulation period, thus making the Rapture and Second Coming the same event.

Premillennialism: Jesus Christ returns to earth before 1,000 years or Millennium and reigns on earth from David's throne in Jerusalem. Predecessor of premillennialism is chiliasm, which means doctrine of the millennium or kingdom age to come. Premillennialism believes there is one thousand years between the first and second resurrection, where David's kingdom will be restored and every earthly covenant with Israel fulfilled.

Preterism: The fourth of four views that seeks to answer the question of when is Revelation fulfilled in history. The other views are idealism, historicism, and futurism. Preterism believes that the Olivet Discourse and Revelation were fulfilled in the first century A.D., particularly with the Roman destruction of Jerusalem in A.D. 70.

Pre-Tribulation Rapture Theory: Teaches that the rapture of the Church in I Thessalonians 4 occurs before the commencement of Daniel's Seventieth Week, also known as the Great Tribulation. During the Tribulation the Church is in heaven to participate in the Judgement Seat of Christ and Marriage of the Lamb. The Church returns with Christ at His Second Coming to earth to defeat Antichrist at Armageddon, enjoy the Marriage Supper of the Lamb and establish the millennial kingdom. Dwight Pentecost says this is the most literal of all the rapture theories.

Prophets: Known also as a "man of God," a prophet had the supernatural ability to foretell and forthtell. In the Old Testament, some of the prophets served as human authors of Scripture, just as apostles did in the New Testament. A true prophet receives his message through direct revelation (2 Peter 1:20-21). They had to be accurate and speak in the Name of the Lord in order to be considered true. In addition to the "writing prophets" (major and minor of the Old Testament, there were oral prophets like Elijah and Elisha. Some of the prophets did "prophetic acts," like Isaiah going barefoot and naked for three years (Isaiah 20:2ff); Jeremiah wearing a yoke of submission to Zedekiah (Jeremiah 27); Ezekiel carrying packed bags around Jerusalem to symbolize Exile (Chapter 12); or Hosea marrying a harlot. Deuteronomy 18:14-19 says:

- A prophet is different from a soothsayer or diviner (verse 14),
- God puts His words in the prophet's mouth (verse 18).
- The prophet speaks all that God commands him to speak (verse 18),
- The people must listen to the message of the prophet. (verse 19)

New Testament prophets did not write Scripture, but they could also foretell and forthtell. It is the apostles who wrote the canon of the New Testament.

Prophecy: Purpose of prophecy was to 1. Testify of Jesus and reveal His glory and 2. Reveal God's will, especially judgement, deliverance, and blessing. Some say that prophecy is just an enhanced form of preaching, and while Bible preaching should be anointed and can have prophetic elements, it is not the same as prophecy itself. The reason is simple: preaching is a proclamation of God's Person and/or purposes using the words of the preacher. Prophecy is a proclamation of God's Person and/or purposes using the words of the Holy Spirit. Prophecy can have a greater anointing upon it than normal preaching as well as impeccable accuracy. The three forms of prophecy include:

1. A declaration of God's will (Amos 3:1-8)
2. A call to repentance (Habakkuk 2:6-8).
3. A threat or promise (Micah 4:1).

Purgatory: (Latin purgatus meaning cleansing). This is a Roman Catholic belief that the souls of the faithful are purged for a time before entering heaven.

Rapture: Prior to Millennium Christ comes for His church. Greek word is harpazo "), to snatch or catch away." The rapture is described in I Thessalonians 4:17. Harpazo is used when Philip was caught away in Acts 8:39 and Paul experienced the same when he was caught up to the third heaven in II Corinthians 12:2, 4.